Rosa Anderson
Mt Zion Missionary Bapt Ch.
Ecorse

6 50

MANUAL FOR SUNDAY SCHOOLS

MANUAL FOR SUNDAY SCHOOLS

*

by

C. L. Dinkins

SECOND
REVISED
EDITION

Christian Education Department

SUNDAY SCHOOL PUBLISHING BOARD
National Baptist Convention, U. S. A., Inc.
330 Charlotte Avenue
Nashville, Tennessee 37201

Printed in the United States of America

Sunday School Publishing Board, Nashville 37201
© 1983 by The Sunday School Publishing Board
All rights reserved
Revised Edition, published 1984
2nd Revised Edition, published 1989
Printed in the United States of America

ISBN: 0-910683-01-8

Library of Congress Catalog Card Number: 84-50335

CONTENTS

List of Illustrations vii
Forward to First Edition ix
Foreword To Revised Edition xi

Chapter I
The Purpose Of The Sunday School 1

Chapter II
Organization Of The Sunday School 7

Chapter III
Organization Of A Departmentalized Sunday School 19

Chapter IV
Standards For The Sunday School Curriculum 25

Chapter V
The Work Of The General Superintendent 30

Chapter VI
Standards For Sunday School Teachers 36

Chapter VII
Enlisting And Training Workers 47

Chapter VIII
The Officers' And Teachers' Meeting 52

Chapter IX
Records and Reports 57

Chapter X
Housing And Equipment For The Sunday School 73

Chapter XI
Publicity And Promotion 89

Chapter XII
The Sunday School In Its Wider Relationships 93

Chapter XIII
Standard Of Excellence For Baptist Sunday Schools 97

Chapter XIV
Calendar Of Activities And Observations
  For The Sunday School 102

APPENDIX
The History Of The National Baptist Congress
  Of Christian Education 107

LIST OF ILLUSTRATIONS

PAGE

Organizational chart for the Board of Christian Education	(9)
Organizational Chart for the Sunday School	(10)
Diagram for a three-division Departmentalized Sunday School	(21)
The Place Of The Bible In Teaching And Life's Experience	(42)
A Suggested Lesson Plan Outline	(43)
Rating Scale For Teachers	(45)
Attendance Chart	(59)
Class Report Card	(60)
Sunday School Class Collection Envelope	(62)
Division Secretary's Composite Report	(64)
General Secretary's Daily Report	(66)
Individual Enrollment And Attendance Card	(67)
Teachers and Officers Record and Attendance Card	(68)
Religious Census By Families	(71)
Floor Plans For Church Buildings Which Accommodate Christian Education Programs	(75-88)

Forward To First Edition

The great faith of the Christian church is that it entrusts its educational program—the perpetuation of its message and teaching—into the hands of non-professional persons who volunteer their services out of their loyalty to God and out of their desire to be a part of the great movement looking forward to the Kingdom of God on earth. In acknowledging its debt of gratitude for this expression of loyalty and devotion on the part of these workers the Christian church owes to them every possible help it can give in assisting them to acquire the skills and techniques and mastery of the programs of the organizations in the church through which they must work.

The most effective organization for Christian education in the church is the Sunday school. Its leaders are products of its program. It reaches more persons with Christian teaching than any single organization in the local church. It has influenced the lives of millions of boys and girls, men and women for good. As an agency for Christian education it must maintain high standards of efficiency and work, realizing that the test of its program is in the lives of the boys and girls, men and women that it serves.

In order to give guidance to Sunday school work and to maintain a standard of Sunday school efficiency in the National Baptist Convention, U.S.A., Inc., the Sunday School Publishing Board has published this manual. This manual goes out with the hope that Sunday schools will adopt the manual as their own and will map out a program aiming at the standards set forth here.

This manual comes out of the experiences of many persons in Sunday school work over a period of years. We express appreciation to all who have in any way made contribution to this manual.

This manual goes forth dedicated to the principle that Christian education is an indispensable aid to the cause of the Kingdom of God, and the Sunday school is the primary agency for Christian education in the church, and that only as we utilize to the fullest all our resources and possibilities in the work can we demonstrate to the world the loyalty and love for Christ.

A. M. Townsend

SUNDAY SCHOOL PUBLISHING BOARD
National Baptist Convention, U.S.A., Inc.

Forward To Revised Edition

When I first came to the office of Director of Christian Education at the Sunday School Publishing Board, I set out to familiarize myself with the Department, the Board, and all the programs and materials produced over the years. One of the pieces of material I came upon was The Manual For Sunday Schools by Dr. Charles L. Dinkins. I discovered it had been written in 1948. Although Dr. Dinkins had prepared the work sometime ago, as I read it thirty years later in 1978, its projections seemed so new and its proposals so necessary. The crisp articulation of the need for Christian education via the Sunday school and the orderly delineation of the structural apparatus to do the work provided the impetus for me to recommend its publication in a revised edition.

In his foreword to the 1948 edition, Dr. A. M. Townsend stated that Christian education at the local church level is generally done by volunteers, Sunday School Superintendents, and teachers. He contended that the mandate before the Sunday School Publishing Board was to provide those persons with the best resources possible in order to do their work. He commended the MANUAL FOR SUNDAY SCHOOLS to this task. It is my judgment that this publication unequivocally continues to be suitable for the task. To my knowledge, no publication has appeared on the Christian education agenda worthy enough to challenge or displace Dr. Dinkins' work of thirty-five years ago. It alone rises up from a common and familiar milieu and addresses the peculiar needs of National Baptists in the formulation of sound Christian education programs and practices in the Sunday school.

In the main, Dr. Dinkins' work has been left intact. Only some minor adjustments in grammar, syntax, and punctuation have been made. However, a major substitution and a vastly important addition have been made. New and up-to-date floor plans for Christian education facilities replace those of the 1948 edition. Placement of those floor plans in the volume purposefully encourages pastors and congregations to incorporate Christian education facilites in their plans for newly constructed or remodeled church structures. The samples herein are new, imaginative, spacious, and attractive for the implementation of Christian education programs in any size congregation. The floor plans have been given as a courtesy of McKissack & McKissack Architects & Engineers, Inc., Morris Memorial Building, 330 Charlotte Avenue, Nashville, Tennessee, 37201. The addition to the volume is an appendix which deals with the history of the National Baptist Congress of Christian Education, which also was written by Dr. Dinkins on the Congress' Seventy-Fifth Year Anniversary.

As Dr. Townsend intimated thirty-five years ago, for Christian education among National Baptists to impact effectively, it must do so at the local church level. In order for this to happen, the volunteers, the superintendents and teachers, who carry on the work must be equipped to do so. It is hoped that this revised edition will continue to serve to this end for many years to come.

Dr. Amos Jones, Jr., Director
Christian Education Department
Sunday School Publishing Board
National Baptist Convention, U.S.A., Inc.

CHAPTER I

THE PURPOSE OF THE SUNDAY SCHOOL

FROM earliest times men have sought means of transferring information from one generation to another. The records of all civilizations show attempts to consolidate information and organize it so it could be used in teaching. The school and the home have always been important agencies for teaching.

Further, all civilizations show attempts to transmit the religious heritage of a people. In the Bible there is evidence of this. In Deuteronomy, parents are instructed to teach their children the commandments of God, and to talk about them in the home, in the street, or wherever they have the opportunity. In other places, notably in 2 Kings, there are references to schools of the prophets where the prophetic leaders of Israel were trained. The synagogue was established as a place for religious instruction in the Hebrew community.

Jesus, from his childhood, attended the Jewish synagogue. There he learned his lessons well. He taught his disciples and left to them and those who were to come after them the commandment to "teach all nations . . . to observe all things . . . ." Just how well the early church followed this command may be seen in the diligence with which they set themselves to the task and the type of persons who developed in the midst of this training and experience.

The modern Sunday school movement had its beginning outside the church. To be sure, there had been religious instruction since the time of Christ. The Catholics instituted the catechumenical system as a training school or class for prospective discipleship. The Reformers felt that prospective disciples needed instruction in the fundamentals of the Christian religion, and this from the New Testament; hence, they organized some schools and classes. But it was Robert Raikes, a Christian layman who, in 1780, initiated and promoted what has now developed into the modern Sunday school movement. His purpose was to teach reading, writing, and morals. The Bible early became an important subject in his curriculum; and with the spread of the movement begun by Raikes, Bible teaching became firmly established. One of the earliest Sunday schools in America was organized in 1793, in New York City, by Katie Ferguson, a Negro woman. In 1824, the American Sunday School Union was organized; in 1832, the National Sunday School Convention was organized, which inaugurated the Uniform Lessons system in 1872, and in 1875 merged into the International Sunday School Association. In 1922, the International Sunday School Association together with the Sunday School Council of Evangelical Denominations merged into the International Council of Religious Education. The various denominations in America have established religious publishing houses and boards of Christian education to promote Sunday school work within their respective communions. The Sunday school is a definite part of the total program of the church today.

The Objectives of Christian Education in Relation to the Sunday School

The most widely used statement of objectives of Christian education is that prepared by the International Council of Religious Education.[1] It is as follows:

Objectives pertaining to:

GOD—Christian education seeks to foster in growing persons a consciousness of God as a reality in human experience and a sense of personal relationship to Him.

JESUS CHRIST—Christian Education seeks to develop in growing persons such an understanding and appreciation of the personality, life, and teachings of Jesus as will lead to experience of him as Savior and Lord, loyalty to Him and His Cause, and will manifest itself in daily life and conduct.

CHRISTLIKE CHARACTER—Christ: an education seeks to foster in growing persons a progressive and continuous development of Christlike character.

CHRISTIAN SOCIAL ORDER—Christian education seeks to develop in growing persons the ability and disposition to participate in and contribute constructively to the building of a social order throughout the world, embodying the ideal of the Fatherhood of God and the brotherhood of man.

CHURCHMANSHIP—Christian education seeks to develop in growing persons the ability and disposition to participate in the organized society of Christians—the church.

CHRISTIAN FAMILY—Christian education seeks to develop in growing persons an appreciation of the meaning and importance of the Christian family and the ability and disposition to participate in and contribute constructively to the life of this primary social group.

CHRISTIAN LIFE PHILOSOPHY—Christian education seeks to lead growing persons into a Christian interpretation of life and the universe; the ability to see in it God's purpose and plan; a life philosophy built on this interpretation.

BIBLE AND OTHER MATERIALS—Christian education seeks to effect in growing persons the assimilation of the best religious experience of the race, pre-eminently that recorded in the Bible, as effective guidance to present experience.

The foregoing statement holds great significance for the Sunday school. Especially does it point up the following:

1. The General Orientation of Sunday School Work

The Sunday school is concerned not only with transmittal of information, but also with the development of personality. Thus, alongside the importance of the "lesson" to be learned is the human being to be changed and developed into Christlike character. The Sunday school must not view its pupils apart from this concept of pupil growth. The individual is exposed in life to a variety of factors, each of which contributes to his mental and social development, and to his philosophy of life. And further, these experiences contribute to his or her spiritual growth, or lack of it. The Sunday school experience, therefore, is a part of his or her total experience. But unlike the others, the Sunday school, as all Christian education agencies, must help to interpret and draw together into a meaningful whole the life experiences of the individual. The Sunday school must not only teach religious truth, but also arouse deeper religious interest and perception. What is taught is not just a "lesson" to be learned, but a way to practical living. Religious teaching must provide the moral and religious insight to improve the life of the pupil.

Alongside the importance of the Sunday school in the development of Christian personality is the Sunday school as an integral part of the organization and work of the church. The entire church is a teaching experience; but the Sunday school, by virtue of its history and past work, is more generally accepted as the teaching arm of the church than any other organization in the church. The church, in order to perpetuate itself, must seek means to win, enlist, and train people in its program and work. These persons must have thorough orientation in the faith and practice of the church.

With such a lofty ideal for Christian education as expressed in the statement of objectives, the Sunday school becomes an agency for spiritual and social uplift. It strives to instruct and inspire pupils who will help to change society and develop it into worth-while Christian patterns. The Sunday school is, therefore, concerned about the communities and the world in which we live.

2. The Sunday School as a Teaching Agency

This point needs further emphasis. In all too many cases, the Sunday school is looked upon as the teaching agency in the church. There are some who have defined the purpose of the Sunday school as "to teach the Bible," and the purpose of the Baptist Training Union or other similar organizaitons as to "train in church membership." In reality, both these aims are present in Sunday school work. One must learn with a purpose for learning to be meaningful; and within the framework of the organization or place where the learning takes place, there should be opportunities for suitable expression.

The church must offer more religious instruction than that given on Sunday. This is clearly seen against a background of total time spent for religious education of the average pupil. The Sunday school, at best offers only one and one-half to two hours religious experience per week, approximately half of which (usually less than half) is given to direct instruction. In order to provide the guidance which growing persons need, more time is needed for Christian education. Teaching in the Sunday school must, therefore, be supplemented by weekday religious instruction and activities through the church.

3. The Sunday School as an Evangelistic Agency

The Sunday school is concerned not only with teaching those who are members of the church, but giving religious instruction to all, with a view that all should participate in this great Christian fellowship. Through its teaching program, the Sunday school is in the position to make an appeal to all persons in the community. Traditionally, Sunday school makes an appeal to children. Through these children it may also make an appeal to parents and other adults in the community.

It has been proven that the most loyal church members are those who have had a background of training in the Sunday school. Furthermore, the vast majority of Sunday school pupils are won to the church. The Sunday school, through its Cradle Roll and Home Departments, can effectively reach out into the membership and give a sense of "belonging" to babies as well as to adults who are unable to come to church. Through the Sunday school visitation program many prospects for membership in the church may be found.

Evangelism does not end with the addition of a name to the church roll or the administering of the ordinance of Christian baptism. Effective evangelism never ends with any individual, but looks forward always to the strengthening of conviction and development through Christian experience into Christlike personality.

4. The Sunday School as a Supplement to Christian Teaching in the Home

The Sunday school is not designed to take the place of the home in the religious development of the individual. Rather, the Sunday school recognizes the place of the home, and seeks to assist in its task. The Sunday school and the home must supplement each other in this task of teaching. The family offers also a place for putting into practical experience precepts taught by the Sunday school. There must be close cooperation between these two agencies if Christian teaching is to be effective.

5. The Place of the Bible in Christian Education

The Bible is the basic textbook for Sunday school work, as for all Christian education. The Statement of Objectives lifts it up for special emphasis over and above other recorded religious experience of the human race. In the Bible we have a record of God and man and their dealings one with the other. In it we have Truth-Eternal, Truth-applicable to every age and time.

To be effective in Sunday school work, the Bible must be recognized as a means to an end rather than an end in itself. Biblical knowledge and appreciation should lead to Christian standards of conduct. Effective teaching leads from Bible fact and truth to practical applications in terms of the present-day thinking and experience of the pupil. Or again, effective teaching may reach back to the Bible for truth to shed light on today's problems and experiences.

6. The Sunday School and Other Character Building Agencies

The Sunday school is a teaching agency of the church. Other character building agencies, such as Boy and Girl Scouts, Y-groups, 4-H clubs, etc., valuable though they may be, do not have as their direct aim active participation in the fellowship of Christian believers—the church. The Sunday school is concerned with the moral development of its pupils; It is also concerned with providing guided experiences in which moral values may find expression. It differs from other character building agencies at the points of orientation; In the individual, in the church, and in the purpose and plan of God for the world.

The Spiritual and Moral Influence of the Sunday School

The spiritual and moral influence of the Sunday school are constantly being emphasized by many of the successful and well adjusted people in the world today. Many of those making outstanding contributions to the world in which we live testify that their motivation and conviction were given to them in Sunday school. In the experience of many people nothing has replaced the impressions made by consecrated Sunday school teachers who, through their study and devotion to God's Word, transmitted their Christian spirit and conviction to those who sat under them. Many persons will remember the Sunday school teacher who often placed the Bible and the Sunday school quarterly aside and spoke to his or her class out of his or her religious experience and faith.

The values of Sunday school have been repeatedly expressed by law enforcement officers. The larger percentage of criminals have not been under the influence of the Sunday school. Seldom are those under such influence led to commit criminal acts. Social workers and group workers point to the value of the Sunday school as a stabilizing and worth-while influence in the life of the people. Physicians and psychiatrists often search for a spark of faith in individuals under their care; both agree that Sunday school scholars and church members are best patients.

The genius of the Sunday school has been that it, as an organization whose leadership is entrusted into the hands of volunteers, has been able to enlist people who have come through its ranks for leadership in its program. The great faith of the church is that it entrusts the perpetuation of its message largely into the hands of Volunteers who out of loyalty and devotion give of their services and seek to qualify and improve themselves for the tasks ahead of them.

Numerous individuals who are making their mark on the world in which we live point with pride to the Sunday school as important and meaningful in their experience. Through such individuals, and through the millions of those who never reach the spotlight, but who have had similar meaningful experiences, the value of the Sunday school is emphasized and the faith of the church in this part of its teaching ministry is justified.

CHAPTER II

ORGANIZATION OF THE SUNDAY SCHOOL

THE success of a Sunday school depends upon the plan for organizing and the effectiveness with which the administration follows this plan. There are factors, including size and distribution of school enrollment, leadership resources, building and equipment, etc., which help to determine the type of organization which is best suited for a particular school. Nevertheless, there are resources in our communities, persons not now reached by the Sunday school, unharnessed leadership, who if enlisted would make a well-organized Sunday school mandatory in every instance.

The Sunday School and the Total Program of the Church

It must be kept in mind that the Sunday school is only one phase of the total educational program of the church (See diagram). Beside it, all the other organizations in the church have something to contribute to the education program. Even the Sunday worship service of the church is in a real sense educational as well as inspirational.

Hence, the Sunday school must fit into the total educational program, and cooperate with all other organizations in the church through the Church Board of Christian Education. This Board is a necessary part of the educational program of the church. No one organization in the church can minister to all the educational needs. There is a great deal of duplication and overlapping which needs to be avoided. New leadership for the whole church needs to be discovered and enlisted. There are many problems, the solutions of which lie outside the province of any one organization itself, but which can be met through cooperative effort and action.

The Sunday school should be represented on the Church Board of Christian Education. The representative(s) should be in position to speak for the Sunday school in matters of policy determination and to interpret for the Sunday school the actions of the Board.

Grading the Sunday School

It is an accepted practice that the Sunday school be organized into three divisions: the Children's, the Young People's, and the Adult Divisions (See Diagram). Within these divisions, grading should be as follows:

CHILDREN'S DIVISION

Cradle Roll, or Nursery—
  Birth to 4 years;
Beginner or Kindergarten—
  4 and 5 years;
Primary—6, 7, and 8 years;
Junior—9, 10, and 11 years.

RECOMMENDED LITERATURE FROM SSPB

Cradle Roll Director

Beginner's Quarterly
Primary Quarterly
Junior Quarterly

YOUNG PEOPLE'S DIVISION

Intermediate—12, 13,
  and 14 years;
Seniors—15, 16,
  and 17 years;
Young People—
  18 to 24 years.

Intermediate Quarterly

Senior Quarterly

Young People's Advanced Bible Quarterly

ADULT DIVISION

Adult—35 years and up;
Home Department.

Adult Quarterly
Persons unable to attend the school

The Sunday school may also provide for leadership training jointly through the Young People's and Adult Division (see Section VII of this manual).

Grading the One-Room School

There are many Sunday schools which meet in buildings without a basement or rooms which can be used for class purposes. Fortunately this type of building is being replaced by buildings with provision for class room

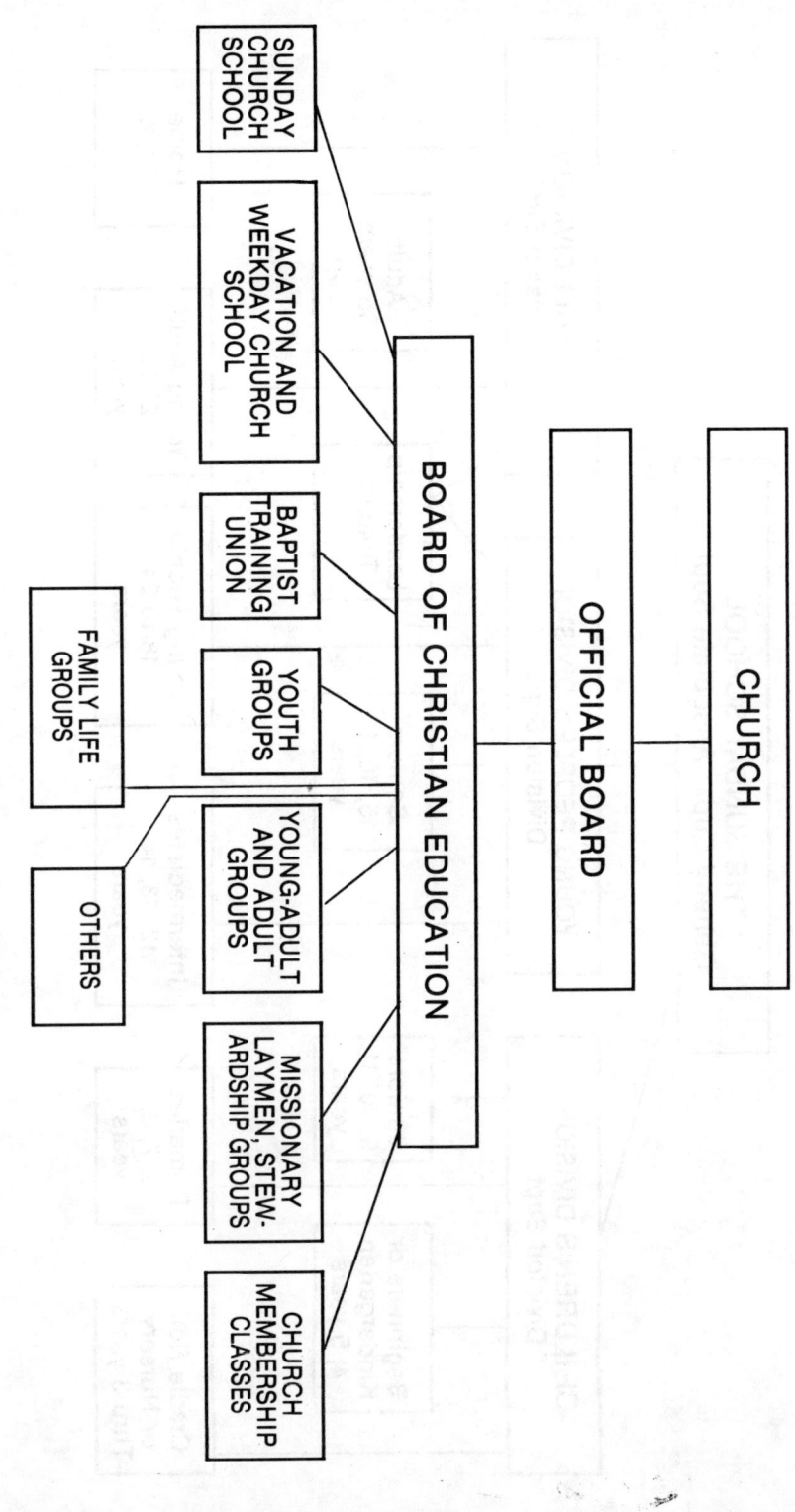

THE SUNDAY SCHOOL AND THE TOTAL PROGRAM OF THE CHURCH

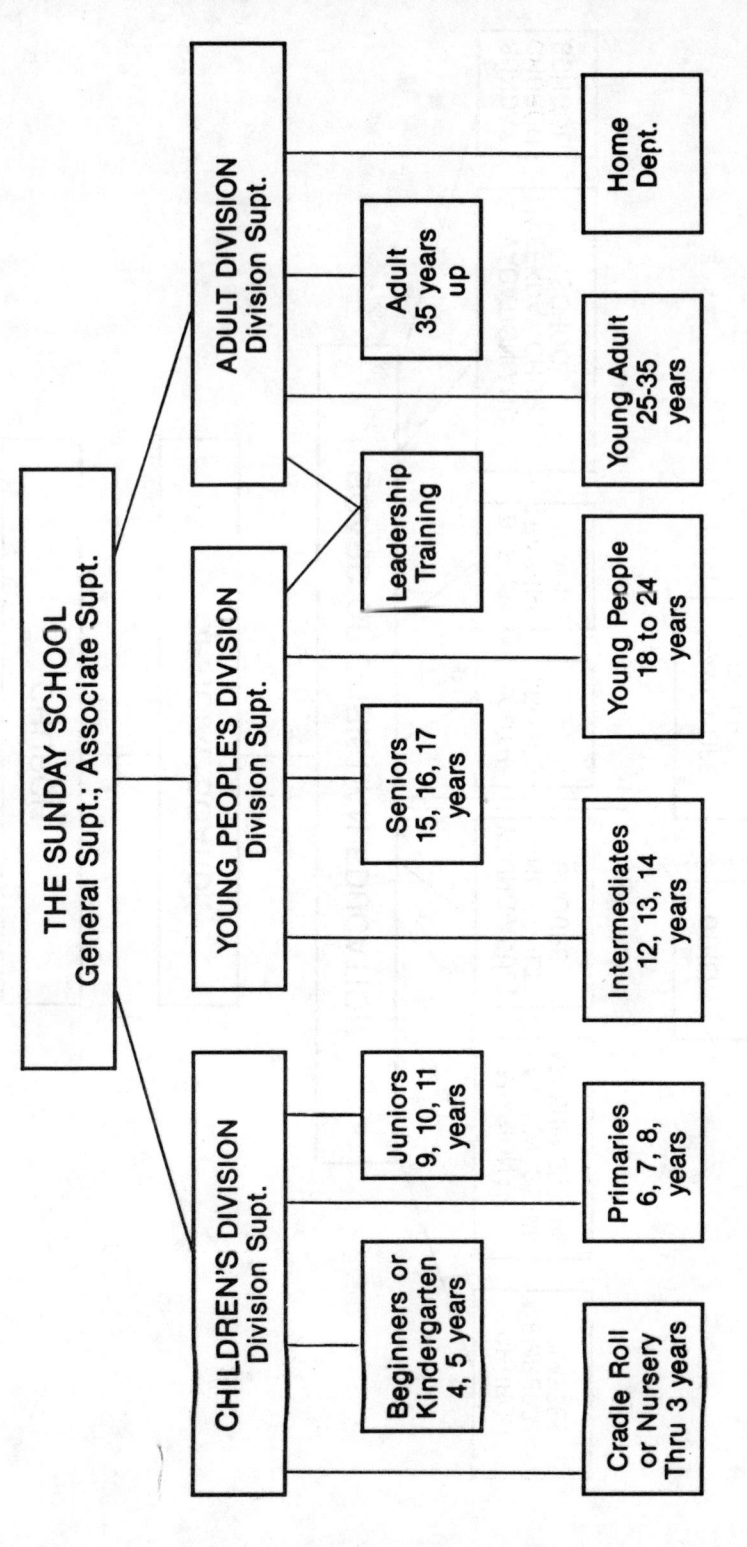

space, or by addition of an educational building or class rooms to the church auditorium. Nevertheless the one-room school still presents a problem to be dealt with.

In case of the one-room school with small enrollment it may be necessary to have only four classes, one for younger children, one for older children, one for young people, one for adults. The building itself may be separated into makeshift rooms with the use of screens or curtains.

It should be understood that such an arrangement is only temporary. As soon as possible (and a Sunday school and church ought to be growing all the time) rooms for educational purposes may be added to the auditorium (perhaps separated by a folding partition), or the church may proceed to build a special annex or educational building for purposes of instruction (See section X of this manual).

Grading the Two-Room School

In some cases where physical facilities are arranged, it is necessary to conduct a two division Sunday school. In such cases, the school may be divided into the Children's Division and the Advanced Division covering both Young People's and Adult Divisions. It should be kept in mind that this is a temporary arrangement, both church and school making every effort to provide for the three-division school with the necessary space and equipment for such.

Promotion Day

The last Sunday in September is designated as Promotion Day when pupils are advanced from one class or division to another on the basis of age. Age, when figuring for promotion, is considered on the basis of what the age of a pupil will be on December 1, following Promotion Day. Thus, if a pupil is eleven years of age on the last Sunday in September, but will be twelve before December 1, following, he should be promoted from the Junior to the Intermediate class.

Officers of the Sunday School

The General Superintendent is the chief executive of the Sunday school. Upon him/her rests the primary responsibility for seeing to it that the school as a whole functions properly. The duties of the General Superintendent are outlined in Section IV of this manual.

The Associate Superintendent should work alongside the general Superintendent, sharing responsibilities and accepting other responsibilities which may be delegated to him/her (See Section IV).

Division Superintendents are made educational supervisors rather than administrators, though they may perform both functions (See Sections III and IV).

A **Recording Secretary** is needed to keep the records of the school, of the officers' and teachers' meetings, to sign orders for funds from the treasury, to order literature and supplies, and perform such other duties of a similar nature as may be delegated.

An **Enrollment Secretary** is needed to keep a check on pupils enrolled throughout the school, attendance, address changes, to send absentee cards, sick cards, or other types of greetings as may be authorized through the general Sunday school organizations.

The Treasurer should hold all monies of the Sunday school, paying out only what is authorized on properly signed vouchers or orders. In many cases, the financial organization of the church eliminates the necessity for a Sunday school treasury, since all the monies raised throughout the church are reported to the general church treasury; disbursements being made according to budget. In some cases, Sunday schools maintain bank accounts, thus providing a check on funds received and disbursed.

A **Chorister and an Organist** should be appointed for the Sunday school. Provision should also be made for a chorister and organist in each division of the school.

A **Librarian** may be appointed to have charge of the Sunday school library including Bibles, books, and equipment which are property of the school.

Teachers who are qualified for their work (see Section VI) should have charge of conducting the Sunday school classes.

In some cases, a **Director of Christian Education** is appointed to have charge and supervision over the total educational program of the church. In such a case the director is responsible for the Sunday school, and should work in close cooperation with the Superintendent and staff.

In a well organized Sunday school there should be a ratio of one staff member (officer or teacher) to teach seven pupils in the school. For example, in a school of 100 persons about 12 or 13 persons should be working in a leadership capacity. Classes in the Children's Division should be limited to about 10 persons; in the Young People's Division, to about 15 persons.

Organized Classes

Sunday schools should provide for organized classes beginning with the Senior class. Class officers should be president, secretary, and treasurer. Provision should be made for weekday meetings of the class for fellowship if not for further study. Advanced Bible classes have been promoted as organized classes for young men and young women.

Scheduling the Sunday Session

The following suggestions for Sunday school schedules are arbitrary as far as beginning and closing times are concerned. They are given in order to provide a basis for the local Sunday school to arrange its own schedule to fit its particular needs. Sunday school may be held before or after the church worship services.

Schedule 1

9:30- 9:45 A.M. Division assembly.
9:45-10:30 A.M. Class period.
10:30-10:50 A.M. Closing assembly.

According to this schedule, the opening assembly in the Children, Youth, and Adult Divisions, will only provide for singing, Scripture reading, prayer, and necessary announcements or remarks.

The closing assembly may be in the Divisions, providing for catechisms or review, special features, announcements and reports, and closing worship (See below).

At least once per month Division closing assemblies may be omitted with the Sunday school as a whole assembling together for special programs or emphasis.

Schedule 2

9:00- 9:30 A.M. Assembly.
9:30-10:15 A.M. Class period.
10:15-10:30 A.M. Division assembly
10:30-10:45 A.M. General assembly.

In this schedule more time is given to the opening of the Division. Thus it may be possible to provide for divisional projects and creative work without taking time from class work.

The assembly periods may be used for learning new songs, Bible passages, special stories, special emphasis projects and observances, closing with a graded worship which draws together the day's experiences. An adaptation of this plan might be one where, instead of the closing worship in the Divisions, the whole school may assemble together for the last ten or fifteen minutes.

Schedule 3

    9:00- 9:30 A.M. Division worship.
    9:30-10:15 A.M. Class period.
    10:15-10:30 A.M. Division assembly.
    10:30-10:45 A.M. General assembly.

This schedule opens the day with worship and provides for both division assembly and general assembly following the class period.

Schedule 4 The Unified Plan

    10:30-12:00 Noon Church service.
    12:05-12:50 P.M. Class period.
    12:55- 1:15 P.M. Closing assembly.

According to this plan the church service takes the place of the opening worship and assembly. This plan is particularly adaptable in small churches. In cases where there is no preaching every Sunday, provision can be made for local leaders to conduct a general worship service for the entire church.

The Opening Assembly Period

This period affords opportunity for learning new songs, for introducing the work of the day, for making special emphasis and conducting divisional projects which may extend over the quarter's study. Responsibility for this period rests in the hands of the Division Superintendent. The following rules will help in planning assembly programs:

1. Do long-range planning, taking into account seasonal emphasis,
2. Exercise care in making assignments and delegating responsibility,
3. Have something meaningful for pupils at their level of experience,
4. Provide opportunity for creative expression on part of pupils,
5. Spend time planning the details of each program,
6. Begin and end on time.

(Further suggestions will be found in Section V.)

The Closing Assembly Period

This period can be one of the most meaningful in the whole Sunday school experience, and can be used in a variety of ways for Christian education (Section V).

In view of the short time afforded in many churches for religious instruction, the closing assembly in the Children and Youth Divisions, especially, can be used to teach pupils material which cannot be covered in the class period, or material unrelated to a particular "lesson." For example, instead of a "review" it may be more profitable for children to learn Bible passages, to become familiar with locating passages in the Bible, to acquire facility in the use of the Bible. Young people may need a better orientation in the meaning of Christian faith and the basis of denominational belief more than they do a "review." They need help with certain problems which they face, the practical application of the Christian faith, and the closing assembly may afford the only opportunity for them to receive this help.

Blackboard illustrations, flannelboard demonstrations, other types of projected and non-projected visual aids can help enliven the assembly periods and make them most meaningful (See Section V).

Committees of the Sunday School

The Sunday school can do effective work through standing committees. These committees should be responsible to the officers' and teachers' meeting. As chief executive of the Sunday school, it is the responsibility of the Superintendent to see that the committees function properly.

Standing Committees

Evangelism

The committee should plan the program of evangelism through the Sunday school (See suggestions below).

Membership

This committee should enlist larger attendance at the Sunday school. The following are some suggestions for this committee:
1. Plan Sunday school enlistment campaigns; urge members of church and Sunday school to report on newcomers to their respective communities.
2. Promote special attendance rally days.
3. Promote competition between classes and divisions in attendance averages.
4. Make strangers and new people feel welcome in the Sunday school.
5. Work in close harmony with the enrollment secretary in noting visitors, membership changes, etc.
6. Follow up sustained absences.
7. Set up membership goals and enlargement campaigns.

8. Distribute invitations to prospective members.
9. Keep in touch with sick members or those who for some cause miss Sunday school; send appropriate cards.
10. Boost the morale of the Sunday school.

Worship

This committee is responsible for planning the worship program of the Sunday school. Each Division Superintendent should be a member of this committee, together with other members of the respective Divisions. This committee could perform, among others, the following duties:

1. Plan worship emphases in the Sunday school, taking into account seasonal and other special emphases,
2. Plan retreats for deepening the spiritual life and conviction of Sunday school leaders,
3. Provide worship literature for distribution,
4. Encourage church attendance and participation in the service,
5. Encourage prayer meeting attendance,
6. Prepare posters, displays, and other visual means of promoting worship in the Sunday school membership,
7. Select appropriate slides, film strips, pictures, and provide other worship aids for the Sunday school.

Publicity

This committee should plan and execute the program of publicity and promotion for the Sunday school (See Selection XI).

Finance

This committee should plan means for encouraging participation in the financial program of the church and Sunday school. Some suggestions for this committee are (see below):

1. To provide for stewardship emphases in the Sunday school,
2. To select some special object for missionary giving through the Sunday school,
3. To encourage larger contributions to the work of the Sunday school and church,
4. To plan special financial appeals and campaigns as may become necessary,
5. To provide for contributions of the Christian education work of the state convention, and of the National Department of Christian Education of the Sunday School Publishing Board, and for

representation in Sunday School conventions, congresses or other organizations,

6. To assist in arranging budget for the Sunday school.

Outreach of the Sunday School

The Sunday school, to be effective, must constantly reach out after and seek to enlist new persons into its program. Some suggestions for outreach follow:

The Cradle Roll Department

This work with babies and small children offers great opportunity to get into the homes of the community and enlist both parents and children for the Sunday school. Names of new babies are sought for The Roll; parents are enlisted in parent education work through the Cradle Roll. By working in close contact with physicians and public health officials, leads can be secured which can be followed up by the Cradle Roll worker.

Cradle Roll work should be carried on both in the home and in the church. Cradle Roll work in the church building includes the Cradle room for smallest babies, and the Nursery class for two and three year olds. Cradle Roll work in the home includes the work of the Cradle Roll visitor in making contacts in the homes, the church, and community; and parent education, which includes giving leaflets, pamphlets and other helps to parents and prospective parents, and the establishment of parent education classes.

The Home Department

The program here is primarily for those members of the church and community who for some reason are unable to come to Sunday school. Home Department work is considered "temporary," always looking forward to a person's return to active participation in the work of the Sunday school. The Home Department can be the connecting link for holding former members in the fellowship of the Sunday school. Home Department work offers one of the finest challenges in the Sunday school program.

Missionary Work

This is frequently referred to as extension work through the Sunday school. The Sunday school through a missionary program can reach out to jails, hospitals, or other places of confinement. Churches with a surplus of trained leaders may help supply workers to train persons for service in churches without trained leaders. Communities may be without churches; the Sunday school may begin extension classes in such neighborhoods. The missionary program can reach out to men on the job, distributing religious literature, encouraging participation in some organized religious program.

Evangelism

The Sunday school can be effective as an arm of evangelism for the church. In this program the following are among the projects which may be undertaken through the Evangelism Committee (see above).
 1. Survey Sunday school for persons who are not members of the church;
 2. Survey the community to find out who and where there are non-Christians,
 3. Plan for decision days in the Sunday school,
 4. Plan a program of visitation evangelism in the community,
    a. Organize a list of prospective members,
    b. Train Sunday school visitors,
    c. Send out workers to campaign,
    d. Tabulate results, and provide for follow-through,
 5. Cooperate in church and community evangelism campaigns,
 6. Distribute evangelistic tracts and literature.

Financing the Sunday School

The following are suggested as ways of financing the Sunday school. Note that in many churches no money is raised through contests, admissions, beggings, etc. Others depend on various means for "raising" money.
 1. Direct appropriation from the general budget of the church,
 2. Contributions from members through classes,
 3. Special offerings and financial rally days,
 4. Promotion of special emphasis days and observances, with contributions solicited,
 5. Gifts from friends in church and community, not regular members of the Sunday school,
 6. Proceeds from sales and agencies of various types,
 7. Contests, concerts, special programs and public meetings where offerings are taken or admission is charged.

CHAPTER III

ORGANIZATION OF A DEPARTMENTALIZED SUNDAY SCHOOL

THERE are Sunday schools which, because of size and facilities are able to organize along departmental lines. These go beyond the organization of the school into three divisions (see last chapter), and subdivide the divisions into departments.

Roughly, as far as organization is concerned, the strictly departmental Sunday school follows much the same general pattern as the Sunday school organized into three divisions. The main difference is that instead of having a class for each age level in the divisions, there are departments, each comprising two or more classes within the same age bracket. In order to see a diagram of a departmentalized Sunday school in perspective, it is only necessary to push the chart of the organized Sunday school one step further, to show classes in relation to the Departments. Note on the diagram for example (on the opposite page), the Primary Department is subdivided into classes.

None but the larger Sunday schools should attempt strict departmental organization. In this plan it is assumed that there will be enough pupils within an age group or departmental level to form two or more classes. If, for example, there are enough pupils to form two or more classes within each of the age levels in the Children's Division, it might be feasible to reorganize along strict departmental lines. And it must also be considered that the space for departmental grouping must be available, either with a departmental assembly room large enough to accommodate classes separated from one another by screen or movable partition or with a departmental assembly room with adequate class room available.

Advantages of a Departmentalized Sunday School

The Departmentalized Sunday school, especially in the Children and Youth's Divisions, has decided advantages. Departmentalization makes possible the grading of the whole Sunday school experience. Worship programs may be arranged to suit the various age groups. Departmental assembly programs may be graded to the needs and interests of the pupils of the various age levels. Departmentalization permits a maximum of integration of the Sunday school experience. For example, if, in a certain lesson for the Junior Department, worship may best be placed after the class work instead of before, such may be done without interfering with the other departments in the work of a particular age group. This includes opportunity for closer supervision of class room instruction than is possible under any other type of arrangement.

Departmentalization in the Sunday school can best suit the needs and interests of the pupils. There are some differences in the needs and experiences of younger and older pupils in the Children's Division. There are differences in need and experiences of Intermediates, Seniors, and Young People in the Youth Division. In departmentalization, help can best be given to meet these specific needs, and the division assembly program need not be "adapted" in the minds of the pupils.

In addition to providing adequate class room space, adequate equipment and teaching materials are needed. The needs are more and varied, and the curriculum of the Sunday school, including lesson materials, creative arts materials, dramatizations, extended class sessions, demands a variety of types of materials and methods to meet their needs. It is best that only larger and better equipped Sunday schools should try organization on a strictly departmental basis.

Leadership Needs in the Departmentalized School

In the Departmentalized school, all of the Sunday school general officers are needed (See Chapter II). General superintendent, associate superintendent, recording secretary, enrollment secretary, treasurer, and librarian should serve for the whole school; greater responsibility is placed upon the Division organization. The Division Superintendent thus becomes the chief executive and administrative officer of the Division, with responsibility for seeing to it that the Division as a Whole functions properly. Many of the duties of the General Superintendent listed in Chapter IV may be adapted to the work of the Division Superintendent.

A Division Recording Secretary and Division Enrollment Secretary are needed to keep proper records of the Division. Their specific functions correspond to the duties of the General Recording Secretary and General

MANUAL FOR SUNDAY SCHOOLS

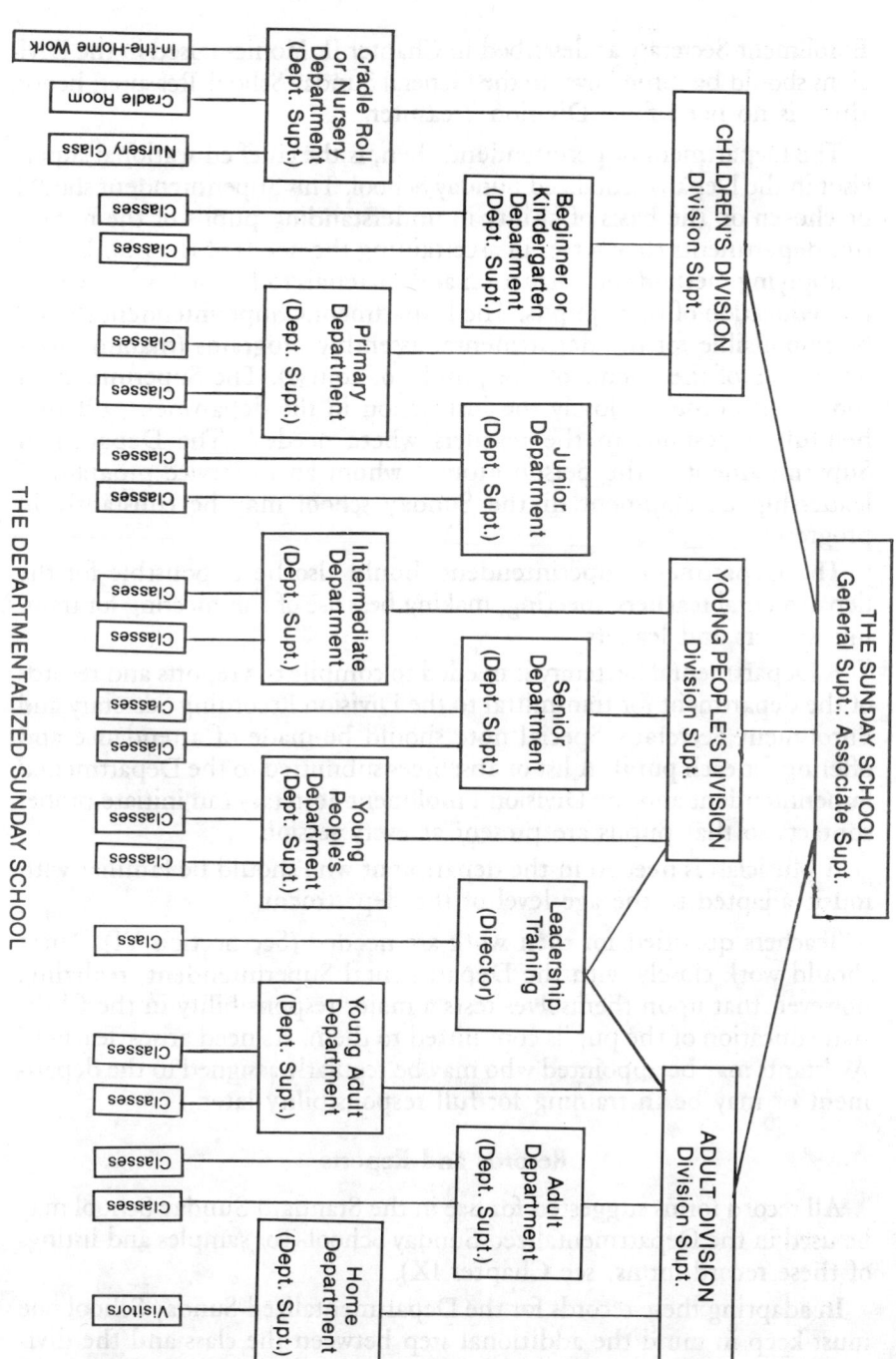

THE DEPARTMENTALIZED SUNDAY SCHOOL

Enrollment Secretary as described in Chapter II. Monies raised in the Divisions should be turned over to the General Sunday School Treasurer; hence, there is no need for a Division Treasurer.

The Department Superintendent, then, is the chief educational supervisor in the Departmentalized Sunday School. This Superintendent should be chosen on the basis of ability in understanding pupils of the respective departments they serve, in ascertaining the needs of the pupils, and in applying methods of instruction and materials to be used in the Christian education of these pupils. The Departmental Superintendent should be responsible for the departmental assembly programs (making maximum use of the talents of the pupils, of course). The Superintendent should also observe closely the instruction in the department, offering helpful suggestions to the teachers where needed. The Department Superintendent is the person around whom an in-service program of leadership development in the Sunday school may be constantly in progress.

The Department Superintendent should also be responsible for the departmental teachers' meeting, making best use of this meeting for training workers and leaders.

A Departmental Secretary is needed to compile the reports and records of the department for transmittal to the Division Recording Secretary and Enrollment Secretary. Special note should be made of attendance and offering for each pupil. A list of absentees submitted to the Departmental Superintendent and the Division Enrollment Secretary can initiate proper contacts so that pupils are present at every session.

A Musician is needed in the department who should be familiar with music adapted to the age level of the department.

Teachers qualified for their work are needed (See Section VI). These should work closely with the Departmental Superintendent, realizing, however, that upon themselves rests a major responsibility in the Christian education of the pupils committed to them. As need arises Teachers' Assistants may be appointed who may be regularly assigned to the department or may be in training for full responsibility later.

Records and Reports

All record forms suggested for use in the Standard Sunday School may be used in the Departmentalized Sunday School (For samples and listings of these record forms, see Chapter IX).

In adapting these records for the Departmentalized Sunday School one must keep in mind the additional step between the class and the division officers. Thus, **in compiling the composite reports the departmental** organization must be recognized.

A procedure is recommended as follows:
  Distribution of Weekly Reports from the class
    Reports to the Department Secretary,
    Class Report Card (2 copies),
    Teacher's Class Book,
    Class Collection Envelope.
Reports from Department Secretary:
  Reports to the Division Recording Secretary,
    Class Report Card for each class,
    Composite Report covering Class Reports (use regular Division Secretary's Composite Report).
Reports From the Division Recording Secretary:
  Reports to the General Recording Secretary,
    Composite Report covering Departmental reports (Use regular Division Secretary's Composite Report, making notation of Departments instead of class reports on the record)
    Offering from the Division.
    Copy of Report from Department Secretaries to Division Secretary.

From these reports, the General Secretaries will compile the report for the day on the regular record form.

The Departmentalized Teachers' Meeting

Many of the suggestions in Chapter VII relating to the Officers' and Teachers' Meeting of the Standard Sunday School are applicable in the Departmentalized Teachers' Meeting. There may be times, monthly or quarterly, when the General Superintendent will bring together the staff of the entire Sunday school to make plans for the school. Ordinarily, a Departmentalized Teachers' Meeting will bring together for general planning those persons related to a particular division of the Sunday school. After necessary business has been transacted, the Departmental Superintendent and workers of that Department should separate themselves for their own meeting.

In this meeting, teachers can make reports to their Department Superintendents. Workers can report on improvements attempted and make plans for their work. They may discuss some crucial problems being faced. They may plan for certain group activities for their pupils, outline general worship suggestions, review audio-visual materials to be used, determine needs in material and equipment for work ahead of them. They may review lesson materials and consider ways of making best use of these materials in the classes.

The Teachers' Meeting should always be pointed and direct. Know where to go and how to get there. Know how to drive to the heart of the problem being faced.

CHAPTER IV

STANDARDS FOR THE SUNDAY SCHOOL CURRICULUM

FOR many teachers and leaders the curriculum of the Sunday school is limited to the lesson materials to be found in the various pupil quarterlies. In reality, these are only a part of the curriculum of the Sunday school. Curriculum includes "All the activities and experiences engaged in by the school and its leaders to secure growth and development in the lives of its pupils." Thus, curriculum includes not only the written materials found in the quarterlies, but also the extra-biblical material used in the class; e.g., Christian biography, audio-visual materials, the experiences of the teacher, the experiences of the pupil, worship, recreation, etc. In reality, the total experiences of the individual pupil are all a part of the curriculum for his Christian growth and development.

For the most part, the basic curriculum, however, is found in the printed materials. Other materials and methods of teaching are used to supplement and make clear the printed "lessons."

Some characteristics of good curriculum materials are:
1. They are Christian Christ-centered and Bible-centered,
2. They are rich in content,
3. They are in harmony with sound educational principles,
4. They are usable,
5. The style and form are good, easily read and understood.

Some areas of content to be included in the total curriculum are:
1. The Bible,
2. Personal Experiences and Faith,
3. Sex, Parenthood and Family,
4. Church Life and Outreach,
5. Social Problems,
6. World Relations,
7. Service and Christian Leadership.

Pupil-Centered Curriculum vs Content-Centered Curriculum

For many years it was believed that the curriculum of Christian education should be wholly content-centered. Thus, the aim of teaching in the Sunday school was to make clear the facts of the Bible, memorizing Bible passages, and interpreting lesson materials. From such biblical and extra-biblical materials, "Lessons" were to be drawn to be taught to the pupils. The curriculum, therefore, was very objective, and the material was to be learned by the pupils.

In more recent years, more emphasis has been placed on the total experiences of the pupils and the development of Christ-like personality. Thus, the curriculum has been determined by the needs of the pupils, rather than the pupils being made to fit into the pattern of the curriculum: And, in this pupil-centered approach the experiences of the pupils have been taken into account. Whereas, in the content-centered curriculum, "lessons" are drawn from biblical and other resource material and learned by the pupil; in the pupil-centered curriculum such biblical and extra-biblical material is selected for study as will meet the needs and problems faced by the pupil.

Classes of Lesson Materials

In general, lesson materials fall into four classes, as follows:

1. Improved Uniform Lessons

In the Improved Uniform Series all the pupils in the Sunday school study the same general lesson, with departmental breakdown of the lesson and selected lesson material for each age group. The grading principle is extended to the Uniform Series by the International Lessons Comittee, which suggests four general age-ranges, with subject and lesson material for each Sunday's lesson study. The publications of the Sunday School Publishing Board are in the Uniform series, group graded in principle for each age-level in the Sunday school.

2. Group Graded Lessons

Group graded lessons, or cycle graded lessons are prepared so that each particular Department of the Sunday school studies a lesson topic different from that studied in other Departments. These lessons are produced by the International Lessons Committee on the Graded Series. In the group graded series, though the outlines are prepared and dated for certain Sundays, each Department studies its own lesson without relation to the other lessons being studied in the school. For example, Primaries may be studying "God Speaks to Us Through Nature," while Juniors are studying "How the Ancient Hebrews Worshipped."

3. Closely Graded Lessons

Closely graded lessons are prepared in units, so that there is a different course of study for each year in the Sunday school. Thus, in the Senior Department, the 15-year olds, will be studying one lesson, the 16-year olds, another, and the 17-years old, a third. The lessons for the most part are undated, several lessons taken together, forming a "unit."

4. Elective Curriculum Materials

These are "courses," not necessarily prepared systematically for the Sunday school. Thus, a Young Adult group may decide to study "Marriage and Home Life," and will assemble lesson materials and helps related to this topic, spreading the study over a determined or undetermined number of class sessions.

Sunday school workers should realize that attitudes in pupils are being formed in the home, at school and in every area of pupil activity. Home experiences and school experiences, therefore, become a definite part of the curriculum of Christian education. In recognition of this fact, the Sunday school teachers should enlist the support of the home, especially, and the school if possible, in the Christian development of the pupil. Pupils should be encouraged to take quarterlies home so that parents can help their Christian development during the week. After all, an hour a week set aside for Christian education is only a small part of the total curriculum of experiences for the pupil.

Some Elements in the Curriculum

The following list of elements in the Sunday school curriculum is by no means exhaustive:

1. The Bible is basic in the curriculum of the Sunday school, whether the content-centered or the pupil-centered approach is used (See Objectives of Christian Education listed in Chapter I).

2. The Quarterlies, or printed lesson materials.
3. Worship, leading to consciousness of relationship to God.
4. Music.
5. Stories, including Christian biography.
6. Service projects.
7. Recreation.
8. Creative Arts and activities.
   a. Drawings.
   b. Dramatizations.
   c. Ceramics.
   d. Writings.
   e. Using paper for blueprinting, spatter painting, etc.
   f. Manual arts.
9. Audio-Visual Materials.
   a. Pictures, posters, charts, diagrams, maps.
   b. Dioramas, picture rolls, flannelgraph.
   c. Visits, field trips.
   d. Recordings.
   e. Projected slides, film strips, sound and silent motion pictures.

In addition to the above, the curriculum should make provision for Stewardship Education and Missionary Education. These emphases can be made in class in connection with the Sunday school lessons or in the general Division or Departmental assembly (see below). Many lessons are "naturals" for these emphases.

Using the Assembly Periods

Assembly periods offer great opportunities for covering much material in the curriculum of the Sunday school not possible to be covered in class. Aside from worship, the following are some activities which may be carried on in the Division assembly periods:

Children's Division
1. Learning Books of the Bible; acquiring ease and facility in the use of the Bible in finding Scriptural selections.
2. Christian biography.
3. Work on specific projects which may extend over two or more Sundays, related to the Sunday school study. For example, making a map of Palestine, or a poster on Helping Others.
4. Pictures and posters related to the day's lesson.
5. Use of visual materials, including flannelgraph or blackboard demonstration, slides or film strip, or motion pictures, related to the lesson or to the quarter's unit.

6. Reports and assignments of Division service projects.
7. Special programs.

Youth Division
1. Forums and Discussions on the meaning of the Christian Faith, Life, Work, etc.
2. Service projects.
3. Use of visual materials (see above).
4. Guest speakers.
5. Projects in creative activity.
6. Special programs.

Adult Division
1. Lesson reviews.
2. Forums and discussions on vital topics.
3. Audio-visual materials (see above).
4. Guest speakers.
5. Special programs and emphasis.

There are times when the whole Sunday school will come together. This will provide a sense of fellowship and "belonging" to the entire school, rather than to just a Department or Division.

Measuring the Curriculum

By what standards shall the curriculum of the Sunday school be measured? Since the aim of the Sunday school is to develop Christ-like personality, the first test of the curriculum will be in the development of the pupils, not only in material "learned," but also in attitude changes, in interests, etc. The curriculum will be filling a definite need in the lives of the pupils if there are definite favorable reactions to it. And, while the pupil is growing and developing the teacher should be doing the same.

CHAPTER V

THE WORK OF THE GENERAL SUPERINTENDENT

THE office of the Superintendent is perhaps the most important in the whole Sunday school. The Superintendent is at once an organizer, an administrator, and a supervisor. The program of the Sunday school as a whole will be formulated around him, and the task of executing the program will certainly rest upon his shoulders.

Qualifications of the Superintendents

It is difficult to set down iron-clad qualifications for the Superintendent, but the following may point up qualities that are desirable.

The Superintendent should be a man of great faith. The Christian religion must be real to him, and prove to be a guiding factor in his life. His life should be consistent, in Christian character. He should be a man of prayer. He should have a consciousness of purpose and the will of God for his life and should see his opportunity for service through the Sunday school in relations to the purpose of God for his life. He must be familiar with the Bible and be of help to others in teaching God's Word.

Since the Superintendent is primarily an administrator, he should have administrative ability. He must see the relationship of the Sunday school to the program of the-church-as-a-whole. He must be able to secure the full cooperation of the pastor and officers of the church and those with whom he works in the Sunday school. He must be a strong willed person, but must never let his will dominate the Sunday school organization. He must know how to formulate programs and projects and how to make them work. He must be able to enlist the cooperation of others in putting over this program.

The Superintendent must know methods of Sunday school organization and Sunday school work in general. He must be able to select the right people for the right tasks and give them every possible assistance in getting the job done. He must know how to promote attendance at the Sunday school, how to keep the Sunday school evangelical as well as a place for instruction. He must know how to effectively utilize the space and equipment at his disposal for Christian education.

Associate Superintendent

The task of keeping a Standard Sunday School functioning will point to the need of an Associate Superintendent to work along-side the General Superintendent of the Sunday school. There are certain duties of the Superintendent which may be shared or divided between the Superintendent and his Associate; also, it is good policy to have someone in training or available so that if for any reason the Superintendent drops out, there will be someone already in the harness to carry on in his place.

In view of the work of the Associate Superintendent, his qualifications should parallel those of the Superintendent. Both should be seekers after new knowledge and insights; the Associate Superintendent should make every possible effort to secure training and to integrate himself into the total program of the Sunday school.

Divisional Superintendents

Divisional Superintendents are needed in order to keep the educational work of the Sunday school up to standard. These Superintendents should be chosen on the basis of ability in the work of the particular Division to which they are assigned and for the help which they can give to the teachers and other workers in the Division. Divisional Superintendents are primarily educational supervisors. They are closer to the real educational work of the Sunday school than the General Superintendent or Associate Superintendent.

However, because of the position the Divisional Superintendent holds in relation to his Division, he also becomes the arm of the general administrative officers of the Sunday school in his Division. Certainly, no planning for the Sunday school as a whole should be done without the Divisional Superintendents; and, no execution of policy should ignore their positions.

Departmental Superintendents

In the Departmentalized Sunday School (see Chapter III), Departmental Superintendents are needed. Their duties are largely as educational supervisors and are outlined in Section III.

Election and Tenure of Office

Because of the importance of the office of the Superintendent, he should be appointed by the church. He is responsible for this phase of the church's teaching program, working in and through an organization. Certainly the organization itself should accept the fact of the Superintendent being elected by the church as representative of the authority that the church has over the Sunday school.

Just how long a term of office for the Superintendent should be must be determined by the church and by local conditions. Ordinarily, the Superintendent will be chosen for a year's term, subject to re-election. Because Superintendents "grow" in the job, change of Superintendents should not be so often as to jeopardize the smooth flow of the Sunday school's organization.

Duties of the Superintendent

The General Superintendent is primarily an organizer and administrator. He should make a study of the conditions existing in the Sunday school and take steps to make the necessary improvements. He should have the school officers and leaders adopt the **Standard of Excellence** of the Sunday School Publishing Board and outline and execute plans toward the achievement of this Standard.

As organizer and administrator he should work in close cooperation with the general administrative staff and the Divisional Superintendents. Here patience is a virtue, for the Superintendent must be able to interpret the overall plans and goals of the Sunday school as they relate to the work of the various Divisons. He should see to it that the records and reports interpreting the progress of the Sunday school move smoothly from the classes through the Divisions to the general administrative officers.

The General Superintendent will, in a large measure, be responsible for choosing and enlisting workers for service in the Sunday school. He should, therefore, lay and execute plans whereby potential leadership for the Sunday school will be brought to his attention. He should analyze the jobs which need to be done in the Sunday school and fit persons into these places of service as needed. He must encourage workers to accept responsibilities in the Sunday school program and be of every possible assistance in helping them "grow" in the tasks assigned to them.

Forming Goals for the Sunday School

The Superintendent will be responsible for formulating goals for the Sunday school. He must see the Sunday school program in perspective, be able to lay plans so that immediate objectives may be attained, and look forward to the attainment of the ultimate objectives of the Sunday school. Because plans for attaining the Standard may have to be laid over a period of years, the Superintendent should be able to set objectives as to what phases of the Standard will be accomplished this year, what phases next year, etc.

The Superintendent should not be satisfied with anything less than the best possible in his Sunday school. This means a regular check-up on the work of the Sunday school, its resources and their use, and the effectiveness of the entire program.

The Workers' Council

Most of the real planning of the Sunday school program will be done in the Workers' Council or in the Officers' and Teachers' Meeting (See Chapter VIII). The General Superintendent will be expected to take leadership here.

The General Assembly

The General Superintendent should preside at the general assemblies of the entire Sunday school. In order that the assembly programs of the Sunday school may be graded, ordinarily, the assemblies should be held on a Divisional basis. But there are times when the entire Sunday school should be assembled for special programs, speakers, reports, business, or for other reasons.

It is suggested that there should be general assemblies following the class periods at least once per month. If this assembly is held on the last Sunday of the month it may be possible to hear the report of the entire Sunday school covering the month. Some schools may wish to plan for a very short general assembly for announcements, reports, and closing prayer each Sunday. If this is the case, such general assemblies should follow the Divisional assemblies and should be well planned and executed so as to preserve time. Time is at a premium as the Sunday school draws to a close.

There may be question as to whether or not there is value in a "review" in the general assemblies. Certainly there is a place for it in some Divisional assemblies where the review can be graded to the age levels of the pupils present, and where various methods of driving home the "lessons," such as blackboard demonstrations, visual aids, programs, pageants, pictures, etc., may be used. But it is difficult to grade a review of the Sunday school lesson so as to interest and apply to all the age levels represented in the Sunday school.

Divisional assemblies offer great opportunities to include in the curriculum of the Sunday school many bits of information of Christian educational value not possible to be covered in class. Thus, a Children's Division assembly may devote time to learning Bible passages, the books of the Bible, how to find passages of Scripture, Christian biography, and other such subjects which the pupils need. Or a Youth Division assembly could provide opportunity for facing many problems which confront youth such as the meaning of the Christian Faith, choosing a vocation, God's purpose for one's life, etc. Divisional assemblies provide opportunity for special projects, such as dramatizations and plays, craft work, forums, discussions, use of projected and non-projected visual aids, etc. The traditional "review" still makes appeal to many Adult Division assemblies, though there are ways of using the Adult assembly to be more of an educational advantage.

The "review" assumes either that the teacher has not taught the lesson well, or that the pupil has not assimilated the material covered; thus, something else is needed to "drive home the lesson." But also, there are many more subjects which need to be included in the Sunday school curriculum for which the assembly periods offer the only time.

Relationships to Church and Community Organizations

The General Superintendent is usually the contact person or go-between in relationships between the Sunday school and the church and the Sunday school and other organizations inside and outside the church. Thus, the Superintendent must be very cooperative with his church and with other organizations. The Superintendent should be a member of the Board of Christian Education in the Church and should interpret the actions of this Board to the Sunday school. He should seek to cooperate with organized Christian education work in the community, district, state, and National Baptist organizations of which his church is a part. He should also cooperate with such interdenominational work as possible.

The Superintendent should give guidance to the Sunday school in the selection of delegates to leadership training schools and enterprises and keep his Sunday school in good standing with leadership training work in his area.

The Superintendent and the Pastor

These should work hand in hand in recognition that the strong church undergirds its preaching with a program of teaching. The pastor should be interested in what goes on in the Sunday school and lend his support at every possible turn to help the program. In turn, the pastor should expect support from the Superintendent and Sunday school.

Promoting Special Days and Emphasis

The Superintendent will, in a large measure, be responsible for promoting special days and emphasis (see Chapter XIV). Special attention should be paid to "natural religious period," such as the periods preceding Christmas and Easter, for evangelistic or other emphasis.

The Superintendent should review the suggested calendar of activities in this manual, and determine which of the observances will receive special attention. He should also provide for periods of missionary, stewardship, evangelistic or other emphasis in the Sunday school. Many of the emphasis and observances can become a part of the regular class work. Others may be made a part of the general assemblies.

Testing the Sunday School

As an administrator, the Superintendent will occasionally need to test the Sunday school program. The following are given as suggestions of what to look for when testing the Sunday school:

1. **Smoothness of organization.** Are workers in their proper places, doing their jobs efficiently?
2. **Progress toward goals of Christian education.** (See Objectives of Christian Education listed in Chapter 1.)
3. **Interest of pupils in their work.** Are they listless, restless, or attentive, learning?
4. **Attitude and conduct changes in pupils.** Has Christian teaching made a difference in the everyday life of the pupils?
5. **Preparation of Teachers.** What special training or experience have the workers and teachers had? Are they using available opportunities for further training? Are teachers prepared when they come before their classes.
6. **Evangelism and Churchmanship.** Do pupils accept Christ through the Sunday school? Do pupils grow in participation in the church's program?
7. **Attainment of Standard.** Is definite progress being made toward the attainment of a Standard Sunday School?

CHAPTER VI

STANDARDS FOR SUNDAY SCHOOL TEACHERS

THE effectiveness of the educational program in the Sunday school depends, to a great extent, on the teacher. We have already seen that the experiences of the teacher are a part of the Sunday school curriculum. The effectiveness of the teacher in his/her task is often the difference between a lesson well learned and a lesson not learned by the pupil. Teaching, guiding the experiences of the pupils, is the chief function of the Sunday school. The effectiveness of a live-wire superintendent and a well organized Sunday school amount to naught without an effective teacher.

The Christian education of boys and girls, men and women, is more and more the total responsibility of the church. Changes in home life have pointed to less direct emphasis in the home on Christian teaching. Opportunities for Christian teaching, even Bible reading, in public schools are becoming fewer and fewer. A well-informed church membership of the future must be rooted in the well-taught membership of the present.

Qualification of a Successful Teacher

While no iron-clad rule for the qualifying of a Sunday school teacher is possible, the successful Sunday school will recognize that there are certain qualities desired in ever Christian teacher. The following points should be kept in mind:

Personal Christian Experience

The successful teacher really teaches himself or herself. Thus, religious experience on the part of the teacher can quicken religious experience in the pupil. This is not to say that the only qualifications of a teacher is to be a "good Christian." The teacher must be convinced of the virtue of Christian faith and experience, and show the same in everyday life.

Knowledge of the Christian Faith

Each Christian teacher lays the foundation for doctrinal belief in his/her pupils. The teacher should be familiar with the biblical doctrines of God, Jesus, the Holy Spirit, Man, Salvation, the Function of the Church, the Future Life, and other doctrinal points, and must have faith he/she can defend and call his/her own.

Faith in the Teaching Task

The teacher must believe in the validity of the teaching aspect of the church's program and be convinced that in teaching he/she is making a contribution to the Kingdom of God. The teacher must believe that pupils can change and that with proper guidance this change can be in the right direction and for constructive ends.

Love of Persons

The teacher must love people, love to work with them, and love to see them growing and developing in Christian personalities.

Training for Teaching

The opportunity for service imposes responsibility. The teacher must know his/her pupils, know the methods of teaching and conducting the class, know how to discover and meet the needs of the pupil, and know how to guide the development of human personality. The teacher must feel that even though he/she is in an active service, he/she is a learner, and should constantly seek opportunities to improve himself/herself and his/her work. The teacher must be able to make sound decisions and to lead pupils to do the same.

Conception of Goal

The teacher must have the knowledge that Christian teaching leads somewhere and must see where he/she fits into this pattern. The goals of Christian teaching include the development of Christian personality as well as the coming of the Kingdom of God; preparation for life here through spiritual enrichment, as well as preparation for eternal life.

Some Things That Make Teaching Successful

1. **Knowledge of the educational program of the church.** Where does the teaching program of the Sunday school fit into the total program of the church? How can the educational program of the Sunday school class be coordinated with the educational program of boys and girls, young adult and adult groups in other organizations of the church?

2. **Regularity and punctuality in attendance.** The teacher cannot do good work with a class if he/she is irregular in attendance, or if he/she does not think enough of the teaching task and the pupils to be punctual, ready to start each Sunday's work.

3. **Thorough preparation of the lesson.** The teacher should be thoroughly prepared for work in the class. This includes knowledge of the "lesson," assignments for pupils, special projects, lead questions or topics, all coordinated into a plan for conducting the class session.

4. **Availability of materials to be used in class work.** As an outcome of the teaching plan, the teacher should know what materials and helps such as Bibles, maps visual aids, etc., will be needed in teaching the lesson, and have these available in the class.

5. **Insight into the needs of the pupils.** The teacher should expect to visit the homes of the pupils, to know the program of the school, and to cooperate with these in meeting the needs of the pupils. Sunday school is not merely a "lesson" to be taught, but a need to be met.

6. **Mastery of teaching methods.** The teacher should know the various methods of teaching and when to use each for maximum effectiveness. The teacher should strive for as much pupil participation as possible in class.

Training for Christian Leadership

There are many opportunities available for training of Christian teachers. These include:

Leadership Education Courses. Courses of the Standard Leadership Curriculum may be taken through the Department of Christian Education of the Sunday School Publishing Board. These courses may be taken in the following way:

1. Through a Local Church Class or School, Church workers' conferences, teachers' meetings, missionary societies, laymen's organizations, local church leadership training schools, and the like, excellent opportunities are offered for work of this sort.
2. Through Community Leadership Schools, where churches may come together to offer courses for the training of their leaders. Ministerial

association Sunday school unions, superintendents' unions, city-wide laymen and women's organizations usually afford good opportunity for promoting such schools.
3. Through District, State, and National Organizations, such as Sunday school congresses and conventions, woman's conventions, laymen's convention, young people's conventions, and through institutes or schools planned or sponsored through district associations and state conventions.

A number of courses are specifically suggested for Sunday school teachers such as:

Early Childhood Development, Primary and Nursery Education

Course	Course No.
1. Foundations of Christian Education	214
2. Ways of Teaching	218
3. Creative Teaching in the Church School	219
4. Storytelling in Christian Education	221
5. Missionary Education for Children	229
6. Dramatics in Christian Education	241
7. The Home and Church Working Together with Children	250
8. One Parent Family	254
9. Understanding Children	256
10. Teaching Children	257
11. The Use of the Bible With Children	260
12. Creative Activities in Guiding Children	261
13. When Children Worship	262
14. Working With Nursery Children	263
15. Working with Kindergarten Children	264
16. Nursery, Beginners and Primary Union	267
17. Dimensions of Christian Leadership	292
18. Administering the Vacation Church School	406
19. Public Speaking	423
20. Christian Ethics	503

Adolescent Development

COURSE	COURSE NO.
1. Biblical Models for Christian Education	213
2. Christian Character and How It Develops	217

3. Way of Teaching 218
4. Creative Teaching in the Church School 219
5. Audio Visual Resources in Christian Education 220
6. Recreational Leadership 222
7. Youth and the World-Wide Mission of the Church 236
8. Dramatics in Christian Education 241
9. The Christian Home 248
10. The Family in the Bible 253
11. Working With Junior Boys and Girls 266
12. The Church's Ministry to Youth 268
13. Understanding Youth 269
14. Peculiarities of Black Youth 270
15. Youth Understanding Themselves 272
16. Teaching Youth 273
17. Helping Young People Develop Christian Beliefs 276
18. Youth at Worship 277
19. Career Planning in Christian Content 278
20. Christian Education and the Black Adolescent 285

Adult Development

Course   Course No.

1. Foundations of Christian Education 214
2. The Educational Task of the Church 216
3. Christian Character and How It Develops 217
4. Ways of Teaching 218
5. Creative Teaching in the Church School 219
6. Christian Education and National Baptists 225
7. Career Planning in Christian Context 278
8. Christian Youth on College Campuses 282
9. Understanding Adults 286
10. Methods and Materials in Adult Education 287.1
11. Christian Education for Adults 287.2
12. Young Adult Work of the Church 288
13. Teaching the Single Adult Christian 289
14. Adult Classes in Sunday School 290
15. Christian Education for Older Adults 291
16. Interfaith Issues 312
17. Administering the Vacation Church School 406
18. Public Speaking 423
19. Christian Ethics 503
20. A Christian View Toward Aging 506

In addition to these courses, teachers in the Children's Division should take courses related to the religious education of children. Teachers in the Young People's Division should take courses related to young people. Teachers in the Adult Division should take courses suitable for the Christian education of adults. Courses should be selected bearing in mind the requirements for Certificates of Progress. Each Sunday school teacher should strive for at least a First Certificate of Progress.

Attendance of Institutes, Laboratory Schools, Workshops, Coaching Conferences. These offer excellent opportunities for informal training for Christian leadership. Usually such training opportunities are to some extent specialized appealing to a particular interest group, or offering a specific type of training.

Visitations. Sunday school teachers can learn much by visiting other Sunday schools, especially those with better teaching programs and from which something can be learned. Here they have opportunity to observe good teaching and make comparisons with their own work. Often "Experts" can be called to criticize the work of the Sunday school teachers, suggesting methods of improving such work.

Supervision. It is the plan of the Standard Sunday School (see Section II of this manual) that there be supervision of teachers at the Divisional level, the Division Superintendent (the Department Superintendent in the Departmentalized Sunday School), being responsible for such supervision. Teachers should be allowed to look to their leaders for helps with teaching problems. An adequate program of supervision may develop into a program of in-service training through the Sunday school.

Special Short Courses. Many Baptist schools and colleges offer special short courses for church workers where Sunday school teachers can receive help. The summer programs and short courses and extension programs of the American Baptist Theological Seminary include provision for such training. Information concerning such activities may be secured by writing the school:

> The American Baptist College of the
> American Baptist Theological Seminary
> 1800 Whites Creek Pike
> Nashville, Tennessee 37207

Preparation for Teaching the Class

A discussion of teaching methods and their uses may be found in any good book on methods. The effective teacher, however, cannot be a slave to teaching methods, but must be creative and must use a variety of teaching methods and procedures.

The following are some points which should be kept in mind in making preparations for teaching the class: What are the characteristics of the pupils to be taught? How do pupils learn? What methods of teaching are best suited for the pupils?

What help can I receive from the quarterlies? What points in the lesson meet the needs of the pupils? What experiences through which the pupils are passing can be used to illustrate points in the lesson? What illustrations from Christian biography are pertinent to the lesson or to the needs of the pupils? What visual materials, arts and crafts, or other creative work, can be used to enrich the lesson experience? What is the relationship of this lesson to the next one? To the quarter's study?

The place of the Bible. The accompanying diagram serves to illustrate the place of the Bible in teaching and the relationship of the Bible to life's experiences.

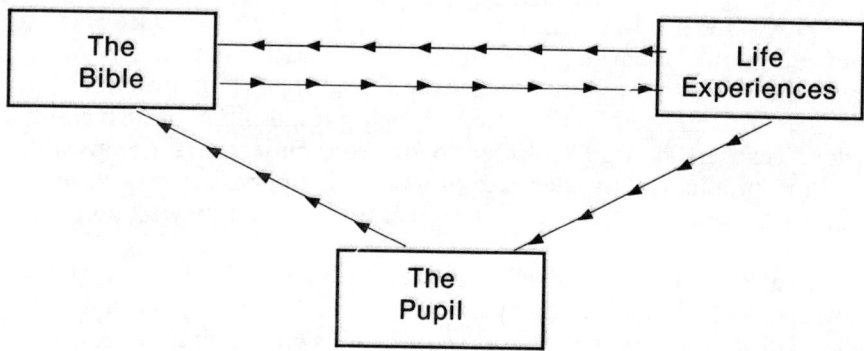

The aim of teaching is the Christian growth and development of the pupil. It is possible to begin either with the Bible or with life's experiences to accomplish this aim. In either case, one must be related to the other.

Thus, the teacher may use the biblical lesson text as the basis for the lesson. But this must be related to the life experiences of the pupil before it has real meaning. Or the teacher may use some life experiences or problem faced by the members of the class as a basis for the lesson. But this must be related to eternal biblical truth if the lesson is to have proper grounding.

A Suggested Lesson Plan Outline. The accompanying diagram suggests a possible lesson plan which will help Sunday school teachers.

Needs of Pupils and Problems Facing Them	In the Lesson	Procedures (Including Materials and Methods To Be Used in the Class)	NOTES
	Points for Emphasis		

To be effective, the points emphasized in the lesson and the procedures used must meet the needs of the pupils and the problems facing them. Thus, if the teacher is concerned about the pupils, the plan for teaching the class will begin with pupil needs. These may be listed on a sheet of paper.

On another sheet of paper, list some of the points for emphasis which seem to arise out of the lesson. Not every lesson point can be covered in the class; so, the teacher has to select from these points for special emphasis those which can meet some of the specific needs of the pupils.

Now, list the needs of pupils to be met and the points for special emphasis in two columns on another piece of paper. Then, decide what procedures will be used in presenting these "points for emphasis," and presenting them in such a way that one point moves naturally into another, thus making the lesson a complete unit.

Now prepare the lesson plan, placing in the diagram in the order to be presented in the class, the points for emphasis. Then, place in the needs of the pupils and the plan for class procedures. This guide to the class session can help it move along smoothly without the teacher wondering what to do next or how to do it.

The teacher who is familiar with the pupils in the class can nearly always tell in advance how the pupils will react to certain points and procedures. Thus, in the space for notes, the teacher may indicate what may be possible pupil reaction, or some additional leads in the procedures used in the class that do not "catch."

Developing Class Spirit and Loyalty

Every teacher wants his or her class to be more than just a place where pupils come to study the lesson. The following are suggested ways in which to develop class spirit and loyalty:

1. Take an active interest in the everyday lives of the pupils. Know who in the class gets on the football team, or who gets a part in a class play, or who receives some recognition and honor. Pupils like teachers who are interested in some of the things they are doing.
2. Provide opportunity to meet the class at times other than Sunday morning. An afternoon or evening when the class can meet or get together will help bring the teacher closer to the class, and may unearth some real problems in the lives of pupils, which the teacher can be of great help.
3. Enter into friendly competition with other classes of the Division or Department. Competition might be on regularity and punctuality in attendance, bringing in new people, contributions, etc.
4. Visit in the homes of the pupils. Know their parents, something about their home life. Enlist the support of the parents in cooperation with the Sunday school.
5. Provide opportunity for good, clean fun, and fellowship.
6. Develop group solidarity through meaningful group worship experiences.

Associate Teacher

It is desirable that apprentice teachers be associated with regular teachers in service. In this manner, classes can have two potential teachers, one who can carry on in case the other is absent. Such a plan provides opportunity for the training of new teachers and for integrating them into the teaching staff of the Sunday school.

The wide-awake Sunday school should have teacher training classes, and refresher courses for veteran teachers. Thus teachers in the Sunday school might spend six months out of the year teaching the class, the other six months in the training class or refresher course. Another set of teachers would spend six months in the course, followed by six months of teaching. Hence, there would be two sets of teachers, one in service and one in training, at all times.

This arrangement makes possible the building of a "teachers' pool," a group of trained and qualified persons who can be called into service as needed. And, since the average service of a Sunday school teacher is less than four years, new teachers, trained, can continually be integrated into service. A church may develop more leaders than are needed in its own Sunday school, these may be used as missionaries to go out and help smaller churches improve their teaching work, training, and leadership. leadership.

A Rating Scale for Teachers

The following rating scale for teachers has been prepared in order to suggest a teacher standard.

	Possible Score	Your Score

1. Worship
   A. Do you attend at least one worship and preaching service a Sunday, unless hindered by some real reason _____5_____ _____
   B. Do you make the worship service of your department in the Sunday church school one of real worship for yourself, and so conduct yourself that you would be willing to have all the pupils follow your example? _____5_____ _____
   C. Do you practice personal fellowship with God, with at least some moments each day dedicated specifically to this purpose? _____5_____ _____

2. Lesson Preparation
   A. Do you devote a minimum of at least one hour a week to lesson preparation, getting thorough understanding of the content for yourself and for your individual pupil? _____12_____ _____
   B. Do you make a written teaching plan to use in the presentation of your lesson? _____8_____ _____

3. A. Do you relate your work to the whole church program, and are you interested in the other church activities of pupils? _____5_____ _____

4. Personal Relationships to Pupils
   A. Do you keep personal information about your pupils, such as address, telephone numbers, birthdays, and so forth, and such information about their work as will give you at all times an accurate picture of each individual? _____5_____ _____

B. Are you a real friend to your pupils, greeting them on the street, playing with them when opportunity offers, visiting them when sick, and taking an interest in their affairs? _____5 _____

C. Do you visit the homes of your pupils at least once a year, and is each absence checked by yourself or some responsible person? _____5 _____

5. Faithful Attendance
   A. Do you regularly attend the Officers' and Teachers' meeting and all departmental meetings? _____10 _____
   B. Are you always present before class time in order to meet the first-comers to your class? _____10 _____
   C. Do you always give ample notice of necessary absence? _____10 _____

6. Growth in Efficiency
   A. Do you read regularly at least one good magazine on your church school work? _____2 _____
   B. Do you make use of your church school library, reading at least one good book annually on your work? _____2 _____
   C. Do you complete one or more courses in leadership training class or school each year?

SCORE:
   90-100   Grade "A" teacher
   80-90   Grade "B" teacher
   70-80   Grade "C" teacher
   60-70   Grade "D" teacher

CHAPTER VII

ENLISTING AND TRAINING WORKERS

IF the Sunday school is to be successful, there must be a program for enlisting and developing leaders for it. Many problems which face the Sunday school can be traced to inadequately trained personnel. Beneath the educational program of the church must be a program of leadership development. When vacancies occur in the staff of the Sunday school, trained workers should be available to fill such vacancies.

Where to Look for Sunday School Workers

The following are suggested as places where prospective Sunday school workers may be found.

1. **In the Church Congregation.** There are many people in the church with specific talents or leadership possibilities who might be enlisted for Sunday school work, who can be further trained for a specific place of service in the Sunday school.
2. **In the Sunday School Classes.** There are young people and adults sufficiently interested in the Sunday school program who could make good leaders.
3. **In the B. T. U.** One of the purposes of the Training Union is to "train in church membership." Through participation in the B. T. U. programs and projects, persons with leadership abilities may be discovered.*
4. **In other Church Groups.**
5. **Among New Member Enlistments.** Persons come into the church who have been active in the programs of the churches of their former

*This has now become the NBC (Nurture for Baptist Churches) Program.

membership. These may be used in the Sunday school program.

It should be remembered that the Sunday school is a part of the total educational program of the church and is responsible for supplying leaders for the program of the church as a whole. The Sunday school superintendent or some one appointed for the purpose should work in cooperation with the local Church Board of Christian Education in this matter of leadership.

Sunday school officers should expect to give all the encouragement and help possible to new recruits for leadership responsibilities. Workers must feel that the superintendents and other workers will "stand by them;" superintendents and leaders should show appreciation for new workers. In presenting the leadership challenge to new workers, the superintendents should be honest in analyzing the job or task for which the worker is being recruited, and should also suggest what helps the new worker may expect to receive in preparing for this task.

Training the Workers

Many of the suggestions already offered for the training of Sunday school teachers (see Section VI) may apply to the training of all the workers in the Sunday school. The following are some methods which may be used:

1. Give them books or point out chapters in books or magazine articles to read.
2. Take them on observation trips to other Sunday schools and groups; be sure they know what to look for and how to analyze what they see.
3. Conduct training classes and institutes for them.
4. Hold Workers' Conferences (see Section VIII).
5. Hold Workers' Retreats, thus providing opportunity for spiritual refreshment.
6. Send them to conferences, congresses, conventions and the like.
7. Give them personal guidance and supervision.
8. Provide for them a plan of systematic reading.
9. Coach them.
10. Provide for them a good Sunday school library, which will include magazines and books which will give them specific help in their tasks.

The Courses of the Standard Leadership Curriculum offered through the Department of Christian Education of the Sunday School Publishing Board, can help all workers in the Sunday school as well as Sunday school teachers. Special groups of courses, in addition to the general basic courses, are offered for Sunday school superintendents, secretaries, supervisors.

and other general officers. Specific leadership courses suggested for pastors (in the educational work of the church), superintendents, and other workers, may be found in **THE Christian Education INFORMER**.

Supervision in the Sunday School

It has already been noted (in Section II) that Division Superintendents are educational supervisors as well as administrators. As Division Superintendents the general educational work in the Divisions comes under their supervision.

Supervisors in the Sunday school are not to be considered as "over" the Sunday school teacher, but as persons who cooperate with the Sunday school teacher in helping to make the Sunday school experience more meaningful and worthwhile for the pupil. Teachers and superintendents who act as supervisors therefore must work together as a team.

The Division Superintendents (see Section IV), should be chosen because of their ability in Christian education work for the particular Divisions they serve. They should be able to give help to the Sunday school workers in the Divisions. They should be able to analyze class room situations and make suggestions for improvement. They should lead the teachers to further growth in Christian service. They should be able to give wise counsel to workers in helping them solve their problems. Not all supervision is done on Sunday morning while classes are in session. Supervisory activities will be carried on throughout the week when the Division Superintendent may have conferences with individual workers, when the officers and teachers meet, and when plans are made for the improvement of class room work.

What Should the Supervisor Look for on a Visit to the Class?

1. **The Pupils.** Are they interested in what is going on? Is their attention on the work of the class? Are they orderly? Are they engaging in activities which contribute to the class as a whole?
2. **The Teacher.** Is he/she familiar with the lesson? Is he/she at home with the group? Can he/she appreciate the experiences of the age-group of the class? Is the lesson planned? Does she use teaching methods effectively? Is the teaching evangelistic and Christ-centered? Are there opportunities for creative or purposeful activity on the part of the pupils? Does he/she dominate the class or work with the pupils?
3. **The Room.** Are adequate seats and work tables of proper size provided? Is the room overcrowded? Is it comfortable (heat, ventilation, light, etc.)? Is it clean and attractive? Are there adequate materials to be used in the projects and activities of the class?

4. **The Curriculum.** Does the work contribute to the aims of Christian education? Are the activities and projects Christian and in line with the study work in the class? Is the Bible effectively used? Does the class work lead to further investigation? Are assignments inspiring and worth-while.

The visit to the class should be followed by a conference with the teacher in which both supervisor and teacher review the work of the class and suggest steps to be taken to improve the class work.

It is not necessary that the class visit initiate the conference between teacher and supervisor. The teacher should take to the supervisor problems on which help is needed, as these problems arise.

The Worker's Library

The Sunday school should provide books, tracts, leaflets, and other helps to workers in service in its program. These may be a part of the Sunday school library. Books and magazines should be selected for the library which will give the workers opportunity for religious growth and development, improvement of skills, understanding of pupils, and a knowledge of the meaning of Christian education and the educational work of the church.

Suggestions for books, magazines, etc., which should be included in the Worker's Library may be secured by writing the Sunday School Publishing Board.

Making the Church Conscious of Leadership Needs

The entire church as well as the Sunday school should be made aware of leadership needs for the Sunday school program. This may be done in ways such as the following:

Recognition Services for Workers in Service. At the beginning of each the Sunday school officers and teachers during the past year. Also the services of these workers may be dedicated to the training of Sunday school services of these workers may be dedicated to the training of Sunday School pupils in Christian development and growth during the coming year. Both recognition and dedication services should be held before the entire church in order to make the church conscious of the work of these persons.

Frequent Presentation of the Challenge for Christian Service. This may be done through sermons, in Sunday school classes, assemblies, and other groups throughout the church.

Public Presentation of Credits and Certificates Earned. When persons have earned a course credit in a leadership training class, or when a Certificate of Progress has been merited, these may be presented publicly in the church to the persons earning them.

Recognition of Sunday School Progress. When officers, teachers, and classes have cooperated in lifting the school to a higher level of attainment and progress (See Standard of Progress in Section XIII), special mention may be made of the importance of trained leadership in helping to accomplish this goal.

CHAPTER VIII

THE OFFICERS' AND TEACHERS' MEETING

THE Officers' and Teachers' Meeting, or the Workers' Conference, is the heart of the administrative aspect of the Sunday school program. Here the general plans for the Sunday school may be laid, the existing program analyzed, goals and objectives set, and specific helps for workers given. Because so many factors affecting the Officers' and Teachers' Meeting differ in various Sunday schools, it must be left up to the local Sunday school to develop its own program according to its needs. This section of the Manual will only make suggestions.

Officers' and Teachers' meetings Should be **Held Weekly.** There are several reasons for this, including the following: Weekly meetings permit sharing of ideas and specific helps on the lesson for the following Sunday (This is on the assumption that the Sunday school is using uniform lesson materials). Weekly meetings permit taking up administrative problems and matters as they arise. Weekly meetings permit leadership training courses in the meetings, thus completing standard courses within a quarter, rather than spreading them out over a year.

In some instances it will be desirable to have weekly meetings of all Sunday school teachers, and monthly meetings of the entire staff of workers in the Sunday school. Thus, weekly meetings would be devoted to lesson planning and leadership training; monthly meetings would be devoted to general planning for the Sunday school.

What Can Be Done in the Meeting?

The following suggestions will point up some emphasis which can be made in the meeting, and what can constitute the program.

Business and Administration
1. Outlines of goals for Sunday school program, based on the Standard of Excellence (See Section XIII).
2. Arrangement of budget and planning for financing the school.
3. Selection of workers to fill needed positions.
4. Selection of representatives to intra-church boards and organizations.
5. Selection of representatives to schools, institutes, congresses, conventions, etc.
6. Selection of representatives to interdenominational agencies and meetings.
7. Planning for fellowship, assembly programs, general worship programs and other such features in the Sunday school.
8. Selection and procuring of materials to be used in the Sunday school program.
9. Formulation of special projects and goals for the Sunday school.
10. Selection of emphasis to be made in the Sunday school (such as, missionary, stewardship, attendance, special days, and the like) and arranging schedule for these emphases.
11. Approval of records of the Sunday school; planning to enlarge the outreach and program of the school.

Educational Program
1. Teacher training classes.
2. Invited guests and speakers.
3. Selection and review of books and other materials for use in the teaching program and in the Sunday school library.
4. General clearance and approval of emphasis in Divisional or Departmental assemblies.
5. Planning special educational projects and emphases.
6. Planning for use of special days and seasons (see Section XIV).

Divisional Meetings
1. Teacher training classes.
2. Formulation of plans and phases in the Division.
3. Sharing of ideas and helps for dealing with problems facing the teachers.
4. Review and criticism of lesson plans.
5. Planning for assembly programs.

6. Planning worship programs for the Division.
7. Outlining of needs in materials and equipment for the work of the Division.
8. Review of special books, magazines, or articles of interest in the Division.

A Time Schedule for the Meeting

Here again, a time schedule depends upon local conditions. The following suggestions are therefore optional:

Schedule 1. A 90-minute meeting providing for leadership training classes in general meeting, with Divisional meetings for review of lesson plans.

    7:30-7:45 p.m. Devotions, or worship.
    7:45-8:00 p.m. Business.
    8:00-8:30 p.m. Speaker, or general topic of interest.
    8:30-9:00 p.m. Divisional meetings, for review of lesson plans.

Here, leadership training work is omitted in the meeting, such activities may be carried on during the Sunday school class period on Sunday morning.

Schedule 2. A 90-minute meeting providing for leadership training classes in general meeting, with Divisional meeting for review of lesson plans.

    7:30-7:45 p.m. Devotions, or worship.
    7:45-8:00 p.m. Business (or speaker if desirable).
    8:00-8:30 p.m. Leadership training classes.
    8:30-9:00 p.m. Review of lesson plans in Divisional meetings.

Note that leadership training classes may be held whether in the general meeting or in a Divisional breakdown, according to the type of courses offered.

Schedule 3. A 90-minute meeting providing for one hour for leadership training.

    7:30-8:00 p.m. Devotions, or worship, and business.
    8:00-9:00 p.m. Leadership training classes.

Schedule 4. A 90-minute meeting allowing one hour for Divisional meetings.

    7:30-8:00 p.m. Devotions or worship, and business (general meeting).
    8:00-9:00 p.m. Divisional meeting for planning, leadership training.

Schedule 5. A 60-minute meeting, allowing for leadership training, either in the general meeting or in Divisional meetings.
  7:30-8:00 p.m. Devotions, or worship, and business.
  8:00-8:30 p.m. Leadership training class.
  (See Schedule 2 above for credit requirements.)

Schedule 6. A 60-minute meeting, allowing for Divisional meetings.
  7:30-8:00 p.m. Devotions or worship, and business.
  8:00-8:30 p.m. Divisional meetings for planning review of lesson plans.

(The Schedules suggested above may also be adapted to fit the needs of the Departmentalized Sunday School as noted in Section III.)

Some Special Considerations

Using the Officers' and Teachers' Meeting for Leadership Training. As already noted, leadership training classes may be a part of the Sunday morning program (note also suggestions in Sections VI and VII), or in the Officers' and Teachers' Meeting.

If the training classes are offered separately for the Division workers, courses may be given in Section 1 of Group II, III, and IV, according to the Division. (Full list and description of courses will be found in the publication **A Manual for Leadership Education and Curriculum Guide.**) This also would permit the general administrative officers to study courses in Group V or Group VI.

(Departmentalized Sunday Schools may wish still further breakdown of courses, making use of courses listed in the various Sections of the Groups. See, **A Manual for Leadership Education and Curriculum Guide.**)

NOTE: Training courses in the Teachers' Meeting offered for credit must be cleared with the Department of Christian Education of the Sunday School Publishing Board through the State Director of Christian Education of the State Convention of which the church is a part. Forms for accrediting the work will be sent upon request. At the close of the course, credits may be earned and course cards given according to the regulations outlined in the Publication, A Manual for Leadership Education and Curriculum Guide (this book can be obtained from the Sunday School Publishing Board).

Review and Criticism of teaching Plans. The Officers' and Teachers' Meeting is not a place to learn what to teach; rather, it is a place to pool ideas and experiences related to the lesson for the mutual benefit of all who participate. Thus, the teacher coming to the meeting should bring a plan for teaching the lesson for the following Sunday. These plans can be discussed and criticized in the meeting. Helpful suggestions may be given which will improve the teaching of the lesson on the following Sunday.

This review of lesson plans should be made in the Division meetings in order that the persons considering the plans may be thinking in terms of the same general age level-the pupils and their needs.

Fellowship in the Teachers' Meeting. Opportunity should be provided from time to time for fellowship activities among officers and teachers. This may be a light repast at some of the meetings, a workers' retreat, dinner, social, or some other such type of activity.

The Pastor and the Teachers' Meeting. In many cases, the responsibility has fallen on the pastor's shoulders to "teach the teachers," and many teachers have come unprepared to the meetings, waiting to be taught. Certainly the pastor should be present in the Officers' and Teachers' Meeting and offer every possible assistance, but the Sunday school officers and teachers should not expect him to carry the whole load of the meeting. The pastor must be present to "set in order those things that are in error." The selection of capable superintendents will help lighten his burden and make for better Officers' and Teachers' Meetings.

A Church Parent-Teacher Organization. As a corollary or outgrowth of the Officers' and Teachers' Meeting there could be developed a Church School P.T.A., or "P.T.A. for Christian Living." Parents, teachers, and officers need to work more closely together, and such an organization would afford ample opportunity. The church school could interpret its program to the parents and enlist the support of these parents for the program. Parents, too, may have good ideas or a point of view needs to be heard; this type of meeting would permit that.

CHAPTER IX

RECORDS AND REPORTS

ACCURATE records and reports are important in the administration of any Sunday school. An effective Sunday school program must be built upon the facts uncovered in the records and reports. The Sunday school needs to know the person it serves. It needs to know whether or not it is effectively reaching the church membership. It needs to build up prospect lists of persons to be reached with Christian teaching. It should keep up with those who attend; know when there are absences and account for these; know the birthdays of its pupils. It should know the qualifications and work of its officers and leaders. It should know the amount of money raised through its program and costs of the program. Records should be able to give a composite picture of the Sunday school.

In order to be effective, accurate records must be kept as close to the individual pupil as possible. The Sunday school needs to know more than that 100 persons were in attendance on a given Sunday; it needs to know the distribution of this attendance in Divisions, Departments, and Classes. It needs to know more than that a given amount of money was raised; it needs to know at what places in the Sunday school this money was raised; It needs to know the distribution of the total enrollment at any given time in order to make plans and preparation for later work. It should be able to keep up with pupils as they move from one class or Department or Division to the next.

An adequate record system for a Sunday school must take into account the needs of the school. Any suggested record system, therefore, must be adapted to the local conditions and the changing needs of the Sunday school. The records suggested in this manual are minimum essentials. Other types of records available may be noted at the close of this Section.

According to International Standards, the Sunday school year begins with the First Sunday in October. This follows Promotion Sunday, the last Sunday in September (see Section XIV), when members of the Sunday school are advanced from one grade or class to the next according to the standards of promotion. Also, planning the Sunday school year to begin in October takes into account the fact that about this same time public schools are opening and pupils are being upgraded according to public school standards. In the Fall, people are settling down after the summer vacations and are planning for the fall, winter and spring months.

Who Should Keep Records

It has already been suggested that there be two secretaries for the Sunday school (see Section II). A Recording Secretary is needed to keep a general record of the Sunday school, of the Officers' and Teachers' Meetings, to sign orders for funds from the treasury, to order literature and supplies, and to perform such other duties of a similar nature as may be delegated. An Enrollment Secretary is needed to keep check on pupils enrolled throughout the school, attendance, address changes, to send absentee cards, sick cards, or other types of greetings as may be authorized through the General Sunday School organization.

In addition to these, the Treasurer should keep accurate records of finances of the Sunday school, and the Superintendent should have a general composite record of the officers and teachers of the Sunday school as a whole.

In the class, the teacher or some responsible person appointed by the teacher should keep the records of the class and make regular reports to the Secretaries. Each Division should have a Secretary who will keep the records of the Division and make the reports to the General Secretaries.

Records to Be Kept By the class

Record of Enrollment, Attendance, and Offering. This record should be kept in the Sunday School Teacher's Class Book of the Sunday School Publishing Board.

Records To Be Kept by the Class

Record of Enrollment, Attendance and Offering. This record should be kept in the Sunday School Teacher's Class Book of the Sunday School Publishing Board.

NAME AND ADDRESS		SUN-DAY	Jan.		Feb.		March		April	
			Att.	Offer.	Att.	Offer.	Att.	Offer.	Att.	Offer.
Age	Birthday	1st								
		2nd								
Name		3rd								
		4th								
Address		5th								
Age	Birthday	1st								
		2nd								
Name		3rd								
		4th								
Address		5th								
Age	Birthday	1st								
		2nd								
Name		3rd								
		4th								
Address		5th								
Age	Birthday	1st								
		2nd								
Name		3rd								
		4th								
Address		5th								
Age	Birthday	1st								
		2nd								
Name		3rd								
		4th								
Address		5th								
Age	Birthday	1st								
		2nd								
Name		3rd								
		4th								
Address		5th								

Fig. 1. Sample Page From Class Book

There is space for the pupil's name, address, age, birthday, and for noting attendance and offering for each Sunday in the year. There is space for thirty names in the book. In addition, names of new scholars and visitors may be recorded.

Daily Class Report Card. This card summarizes the records of the class on a given Sunday, showing total on roll, number present, on time, visitors, new pupils, pupils dropped, offering, number contributing, number who prepared lesson and number who will attend church. On the reverse side is space for recording names of new pupils and pupils dropped. Excessive absences without excuse is sufficient cause to drop the name of a pupil from the enrollment of the class.

CLASS REPORT CARD

_____ Divison (or Department)

_____ Class. Date _____

Enrollment _____	Offering _____
Present _____	No. Contributing _____
On Time _____	Prepared Lesson _____
Visitors _____	Attend Church _____
No. New Pupils _____	_____ Teacher
No. Pupils Dropped _____	
Enrollment at End of Class _____	_____ Class Secretary
	_____

Turn This Card in Each Sunday to Your Division (or Department) Secretary

Fig. 2A. Class Report Card.

REVERSE SIDE

New Pupils:

NAME	ADDRESS	Tel. No.	Age	Birthday

Pupil's Dropped:

NAME	ADDRESS	REMARKS

(over)

Fig. 2B. Class Report Card (Reverse Side)

Class Collection Envelope. The offering taken in the class should be placed in a class Collection Envelope. This envelope is arranged so that it can be used for three months with a space for record of offerings being made on the outside of the envelope each Sunday.

SUNDAY SCHOOL CLASS COLLECTION ENVELOPE

CLASS _____ QUARTER

_____ TEACHER

_____ SUNDAY SCHOOL

Sunday	Date	Enrolled	Pres.	Absent	Visitors	Collection
1ST						
2ND						
3RD						
4TH						
5TH						
6TH						
7TH						
8TH						
9TH						
10TH						
11TH						
12TH						
13TH						
TOTAL						

Fig 3. Class Collection Envelope

Class Attendance Roll or Chart. Attendance in the class can often be stimulated by an attendance roll placed on the class room wall. Gummed stars of various colors can be placed beside the name in spaces indicated for various Sundays to denote those present and on time, present but late, excused absence, or absent.

Disposition of Records. The following records each Sunday should be turned over to the Division Secretary. (In the case of the Departmentalized Sunday school, see Section III of this Manual.)

Teacher's Class Book

Daily Class Report Card (2 copies)

Class Collection Envelope

(Teacher's Class Book should be turned in so individual record of enrollments may be made by the Enrollment Secretary. See below.)

Records to Be Kept by Division Secretary

The Division Secretary will receive the following reports from each class in the Division:

Teacher's Class Book

Daily Class Report Card (2 Copies)

Class Collection Envelope

Composite Division Report. From these records the Division Secretary will be able to arrange a Composite Division Report in duplicate, for each Sunday, recording on a single sheet the reports which come in from class, noting totals.

The General Enrollment Secretary should receive the Teacher's Class Book for each class. This Secretary should maintain the following records:

Individual Enrollment and Attendance Record. From the Class Book, information for this record should be taken. On this record card is space for the name, address, and telephone number of the pupil. Also, it can be recorded whether the pupil is a church member, whether parents are church members, date the pupil entered the school, date the pupil was dropped from the record, and the reason dropped. There is a space for remarks.

At the bottom is space for the Enrollment Secretary to punch or mark out the Sundays the pupil was in attendance so that only absences will show on the card. This record card should be renewed annually at the beginning of the Sunday school year, October 1.

DIVISION SECRETARY'S COMPOSITE REPORT

Division _____ Date _____

Class	Enroll-ment	Pres-ant	On Time	Visi-tors	New Pupils	Pupils Dropped	Corrected Enr.	Prep. Lesson	Attend. Ch.	No. Contr.	Offer-ing
TOTAL											

Officers and Teachers Present _____

_____ DIV. SECRETARY

Fig. 1. Sample Page From Class Book.

The Division Secretary will retain one copy of the Daily Class Report Card from each class, the other being transmitted to the General Secretaries of the Sunday school.

Disposition of Records. The Division Secretary will turn in to the General Secretaries the following records;
Teacher's Class Book for each class
Daily Class Report for each class
Class Collection Envelope containing money raised in the Division and record of same
Composite Division Report.

Records Kept by General Secretaries

The General Secretaries will receive the following reports from each Division:
Teacher's Class Book for each class
Daily Class Report Card for each class
Class Collection Envelope from the Division
Composite Division Report.

General Secretary's Daily Report. From these records the General Recording Secretary can make a report of the entire Sunday school. This report should be kept in a bound book. Space is allowed for reporting enrollment, attendance, record of visitors and offering from each class and division, with a summary of total enrollment of the school, total attendance, visitors present, offering, officers and teachers present, and offering and attendance for the previous Sunday.

Record of Monies Turned in to the Treasury. The General Recording Secretary should record money turned into the treasury (whether the Sunday school has a treasury or whether money is deposited in the church treasury).

Record of Monies Expended by the Sunday school. The General Recording Secretary should keep an accurate record of monies requisitioned from the treasury, showing balances in treasury at intervals.

GENERAL SECRETARY'S DAILY REPORT

DATE _____

Children's Division					Young People's Division					Adult Division			
Class	Enroll-ment	Present	Visitors	Offering	Class	Enroll-ment	Present	Visitors	Offering	Enroll-ment	Present	Visitors	Offering
Totals													

Summary:

Total Enrollment _____
Total Present _____
Visitors _____
Offering _____
Officers and Teachers Present _____

Attendance Last Sunday _____
Offering Last Sunday _____

_____
Secretary

INDIVIDUAL ENROLLMENT AND ATTENDANCE CARD

On the reverse side of this card is spacing for recording special qualities or talents of the pupils, and for recording activities in which the pupil has been engaged in the Sunday school. This information, which should

_____

_____ Division (Department)

_____ Class

Name _____

Address _____ Tel. No. _____

Church Member? _____ Parents Church Members? _____

Remarks _____

Date Entered _____ Date Dropped _____

Reason Dropped _____

October 1 2 3 4 5	January 1 2 3 4 5	April 1 2 3 4 5	July 1 2 3 4 5
November 1 2 3 4 5	February 1 2 3 4 5	May 1 2 3 4 5	August 1 2 3 4 5
December 1 2 3 4 5	March 1 2 3 4 5	June 1 2 3 4 5	September 1 2 3 4 5

OVER

Fig. 6A Individual Enrollment and Attendance Card

REVERSE SIDE

Special Qualities or Talents: Activities Record:

Fig. 6B. Individual Enrollment and Attendance Card (Reverse Side)

be transferred annually from one card to the next, can give the teacher a good picture of the pupil in his class.

Teachers' and Officers' Record and Attendance Card. This is an important record, showing the name, address and telephone number for each officer and teacher in the Sunday school. In addition is a record of position held in the Sunday school, leadership training credits earned, Certificates of Progress earned, other leadership training, including books read, meetings attended, etc.

**TEACHERS AND OFFICERS
RECORD AND ATTENDANCE CARD**

Name _____

Address _____ Tel. No. _____ _____

_____ Division _____ Class

Leadership Training Credits Earned: _____

Other Leadership Training _____

_____

Certificates of Progress Earned (give dates): First _____

Second _____ Third _____

October 1 2 3 4 5   January 1 2 3 4 5   April 1 2 3 4 5   July 1 2 3 4 5
November 1 2 3 4 5 February 1 2 3 4 5 May 1 2 3 4 5   August 1 2 3 4 5
December 1 2 3 4 5 March 1 2 3 4 5   June 1 2 3 4 5   September 1 2 3 4 5

OVER

Fig. 7A. Teachers' and Officers' Record and Attendance Card

REVERSE SIDE

Record of Service:

Dates	Position	Remarks

OVER

Fig. 7B. Teachers and Officers' Record and Attendance Card (Reverse Side)

At the bottom of this card is space for the Enrollment Secretary to punch or mark out the Sundays the teacher or officer was in attendance, so that only absences will show on the card. This card should be renewed annually at the beginning of the Sunday school year, October 1.

On the reverse side is space for recording the service of the person. There is space for dates of service, position held, and remarks concerning same.

Disposition of These Records. From these Records the Enrollment Secretary can tell those who are absent, consequently wno should receive absentee cards, sick cards, or other greetings from the Sunday school. The Enrollment Secretary should send these messages from the Sunday school. (In addition, Individual classes, teachers, or Divisions may desire to send message.) The Enrollment Secretary can report to the Division officer and to convey the teachers the records of pupils throughout the Sunday school.

Records to Be Kept by Superintendent

The Superintendent should be interested in keeping his own records of the Sunday School. **The Superintendent's Guide and Record** has been prepared by the Sunday School Publishing Board for this purpose. The following records may be kept in this book.

Names and Addresses of Sunday School Workers. There is space for recording names, addresses, positions held, telephone numbers and birthdays, for each worker.

Attendance at Teacher's and Officers' Meeting and at Sunday School. This may be recorded weekly, teachers' meeting attendance being recorded in relationship to the Sunday School session on the following Sunday.

A Sunday's Record. The Superintendent should record the officers and teachers present, number of pupils present, visitors present, number of workers present at the previous teachers' meeting, offering and expenditures, and certain remarks or memoranda which he wishes.

These records are for the Superintendent's personal use and should not be confused with the general Sunday school records. Division Superintendents should keep similar records covering their Divisons.

Other Records Needed

Community Census. The Sunday school should have a record of the community which it serves. In cooperation with other churches, or as a project of its own, a census of the community can be taken, giving opportunity to know who is in the community, their church affiliations or preferences, whether or not the family or children attend Sunday school, etc. From such a record a list of prospective pupils for the Sunday school may be taken.

Report to the Church. The Sunday school should make regualr reports to the church either monthly, quarterly, or annually, according to the methods prescribed by the church. In some cases where there is a Board of Christian Education the reports will be made there and included in the general report of the Board to the church. In other cases, the Sunday school may be required to report through other designated committees, or directly to the church and its officers.

Such a report should not only cover the attendance and money raised in the Sunday school, but should also cover the general work of the Sunday school, its strengths and weaknesses, and point out places where the church as a whole can be of greater help to this part of its teaching program.

The Treasurer should keep an accurate record of all funds which come into his possession and the disposition of same.

Supplementary Records

The records suggested above constitute minimum essentials for the Sunday school. Some Sunday schools may desire to keep other records in addition. The following records have been prepared and are available.

Pupils Registration Blank
Pupils Enrollment Blank
Transfer Blank
Follow-up-Blank
Report to Parents
Report to Public School
Leader's Record of Individual Pupil

RELIGIOUS CENSUS BY FAMILIES

Date _____

1. Family Name _____
2. Street or Road _____
3. P. O. Address _____
4. Neighborhood _____
Village _____
5. Resident of this community since _____
6. Resident of this farm since _____
7. Owner _____ 8. Tenant _____
9. Distance from church: Miles _____ Blocks _____
10. County _____

Give Name	11. Birthday	Church Affiliation			Attendance		17. See Key			18. Occupation
		12. Present Membership	13. Preference Denomination Church	14. Name Church	15. Name S.S.	16. Last Time				
						Church	Sun. S	I	II	III
19. Father										
20. Mother										
21. Children										
1										
2										
3										
4										

22. Others in household	Relationship										
1											
2											

*Key: Enter appropriate letters in columns
I. (a) Officer in church. (b) Church School officer-teacher. (c) Desire to unite with church. (d) Willing to work. (e) Not interested.
II. (a) Grade school—1-2-3-4-5-6-7-8. (b) High school—1-2-3-4. (c) College —1-2-3-4. (d) Name other schools and years attended _____
III. Veteran—X.

23. Canvasser _____

24. Do you have a Bible in your home? Yes ( ) No ( )

25. What passages have you read within the past month? _____

26. What grace do you use at the table before meals? _____

27. Who leads in family prayer? Father ( ) Mother ( ) Children ( )

28. Date

Date	Record of Pastoral calls

Sample copies of this card and prices for quantities may be secured from the Sunday School Publishing Board, U.S.A., Inc. Mrs. C. N. Adkins, Executive Director, 330 Charlotte Avenue, Nashville, Tennessee 37201.

CHAPTER X

HOUSING AND EQUIPMENT FOR THE SUNDAY SCHOOL

IT is recognized by the Sunday school workers that housing and equipment are an integral part of the curriculum of Christian education. The best work cannot be done in buildings which are unsuited for teaching purposes, and without adequate equipment and materials to carry on an effective program.

It must be realized, however, that buildings and equipment must take into account the needs of the church and Sunday school. Buildings must be related to the size and attendance of the church and Sunday school, the type of program carried on, whether or not the program of the church is church-centered, or held in the church building, the type of community served by the church, the mobility of the population, and the ability of the people to underwrite the financing of a program carried on in the building. The equipment for the building must be related to the program carried on in the building, the various uses to which the building is put, the needs of the various age-groups, etc.

Some Plans for Church Buildings

No church should consider building without securing the services of a recognized architect and contractor. Using those firms experienced in building and remodeling churches is best.

The services of the McKissack and McKissack Architectural Firm are available to all churches which call upon them. This firm provided the design for the Morris Memorial Building, home of the Sunday School

Publishing Board, 330 Charlotte Avenue, Nashville, Tennessee, 37201. It continues to offer consultation and other services to churches in the National Baptist Convention, U.S.A., Inc., who are planning church building or remodeling programs. For information, write, McKissack & McKissack Architectural Firm, 330 Charlotte Avenue, Nashville, Tennessee, 37201.

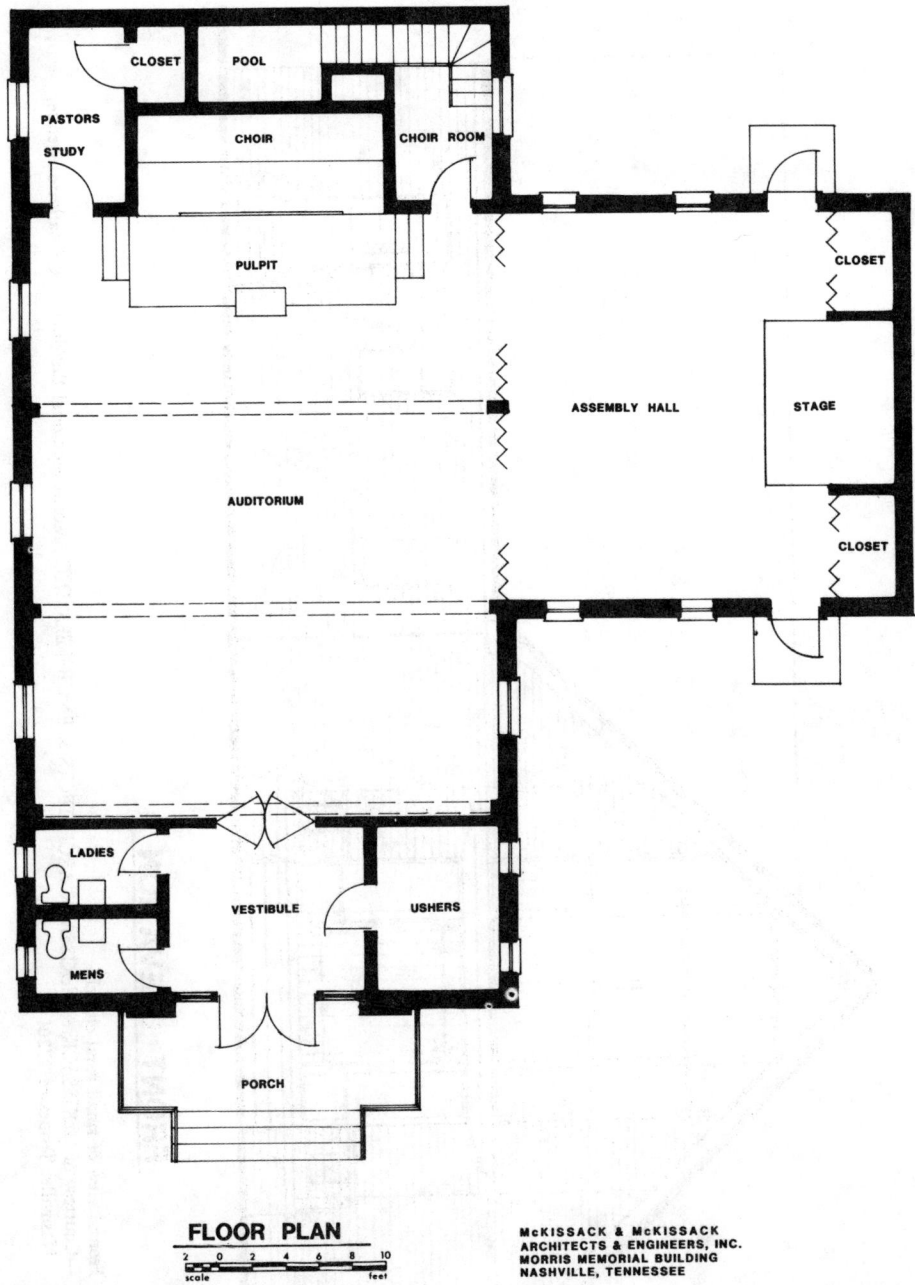

Fig. 1A—Economically designed small rural church. Auditorium has seating capacity of 100-150. A multipurpose room provides space for general assembly and classrooms.

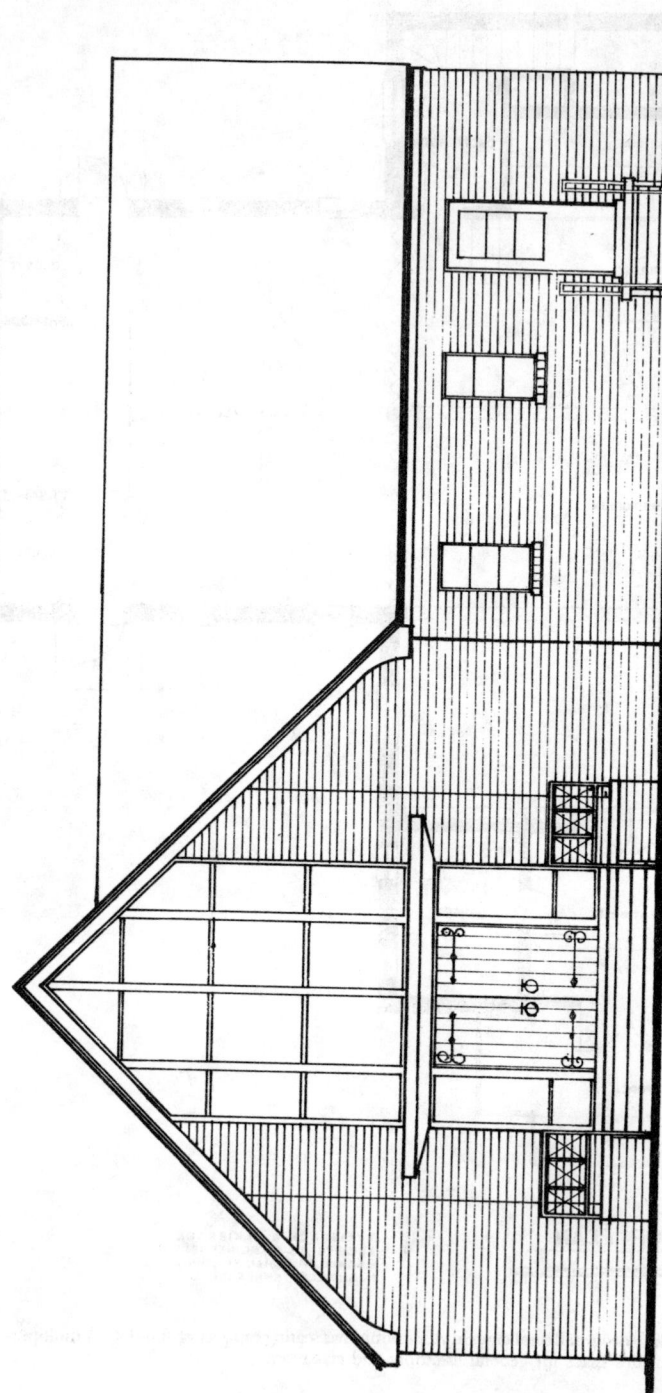

Fig. 1B—Frontal view of small rural church.
—Courtesy of McKISSACK & McKISSACK ARCHITECTS & ENGINEERS, INC., Morris Memorial Building, 330 Charlotte Avenue, Nashville, Tennessee 37201

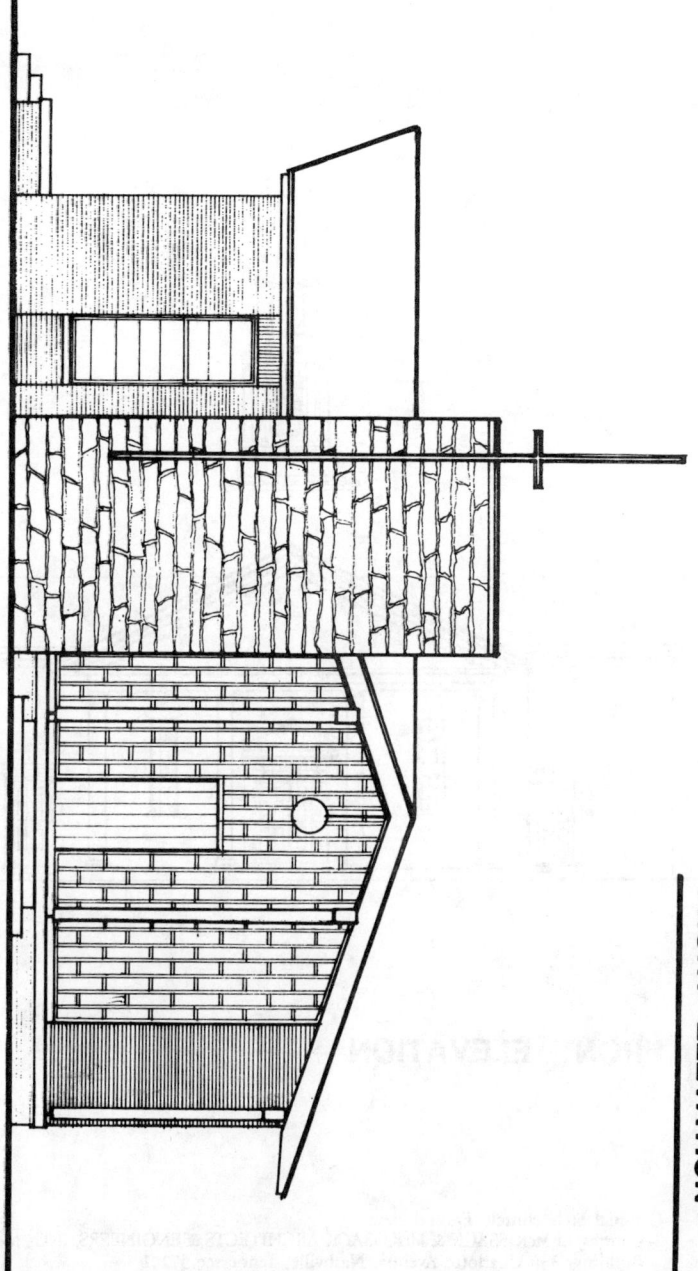

Fig. 2—Frontal view of the Mod Style Urban/Suburban church.
—Courtesy of McKISSACK & McKISSACK ARCHITECTS & ENGINEERS, INC.

FRONT ELEVATION

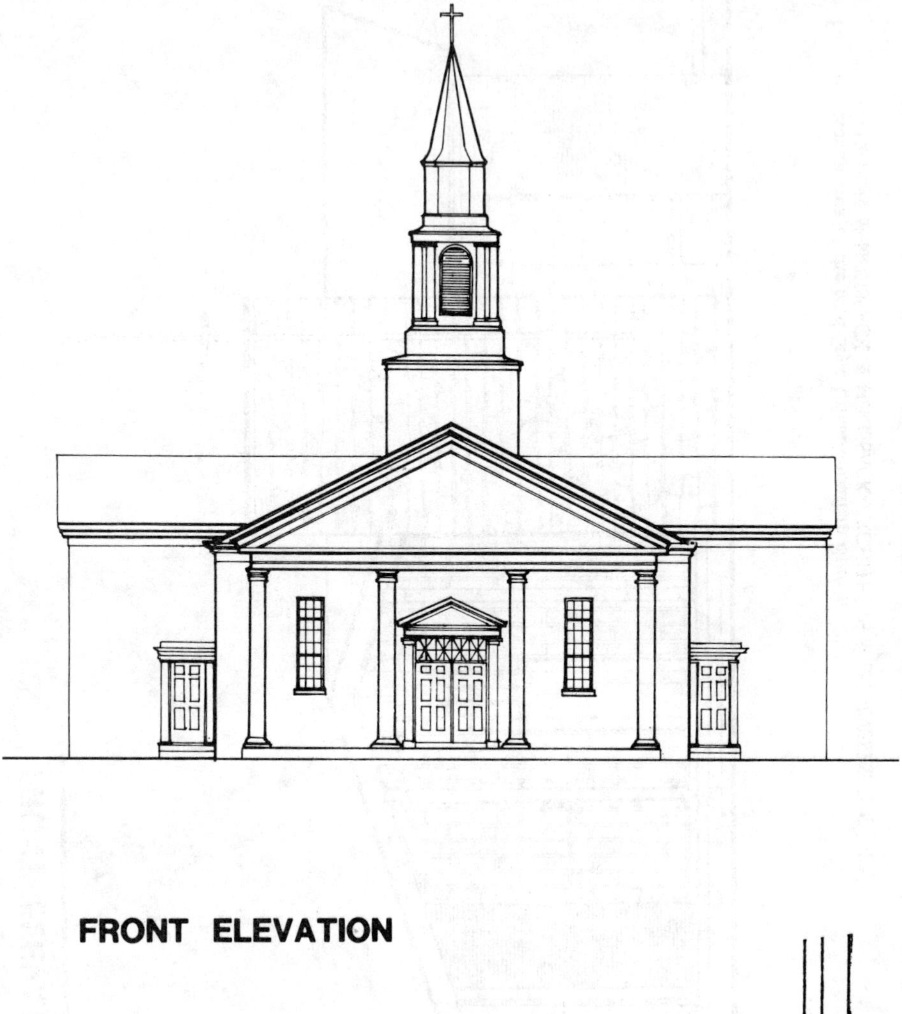

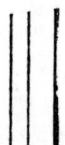

FRONT ELEVATION

Fig. 3 —**Colonial Style church.** Frontal view.
  —Courtesy of McKISSACK & McKISSACK ARCHITECTS & ENGINEERS, INC., Morris Memorial Building, 330 Charlotte Avenue, Nashville, Tennessee 37201

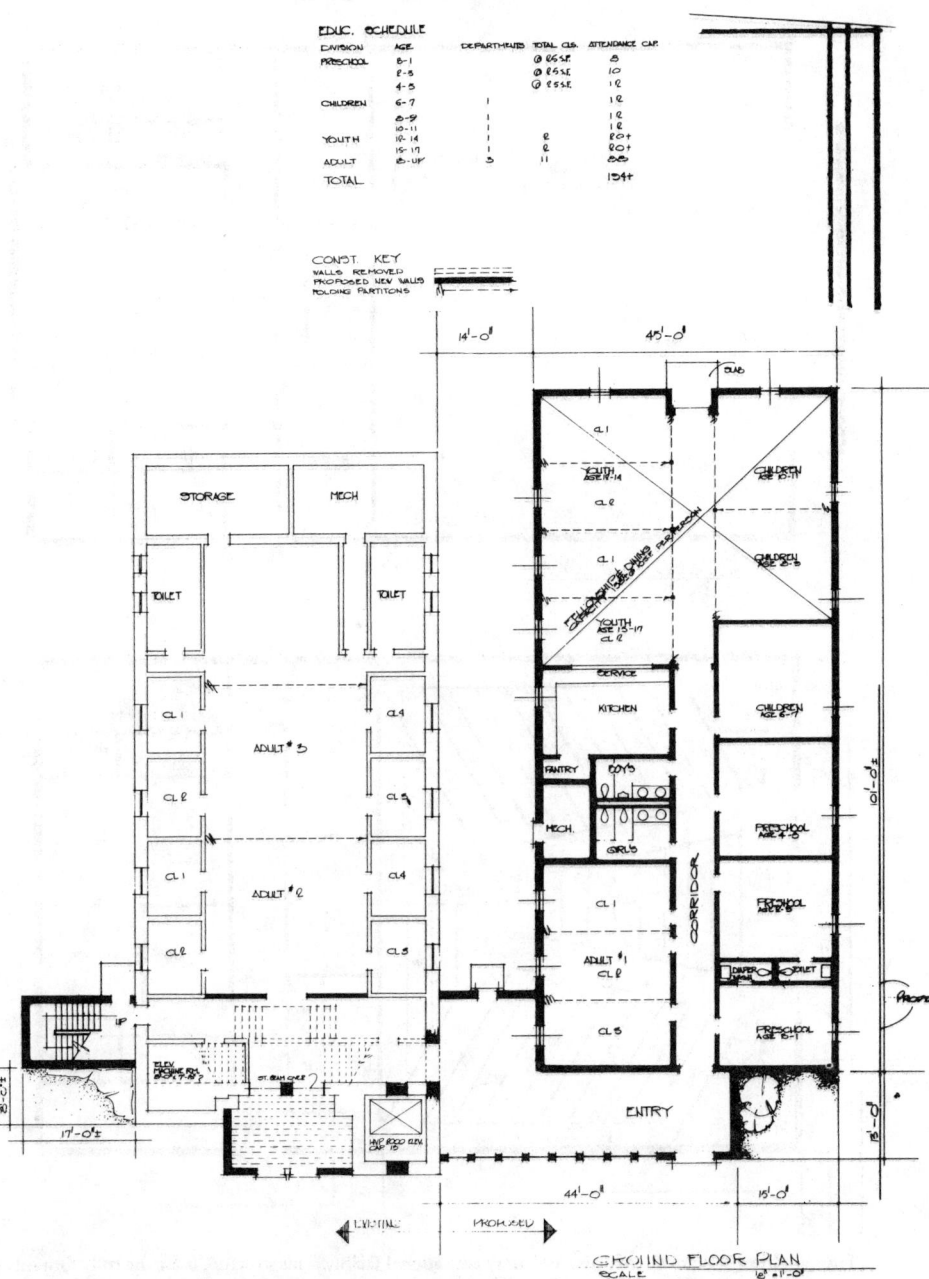

Fig. 4.—**Sunday School addition.** This facility is designed for the congregation that is heavily involved in Christian education. On ground level, there is a chapel surrounded by classrooms and a nursery. The second level has an abundance of classrooms.

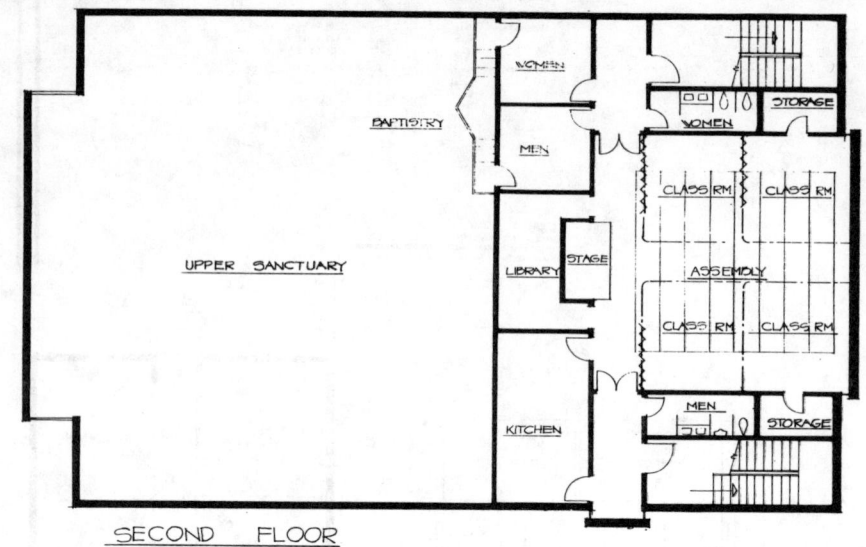

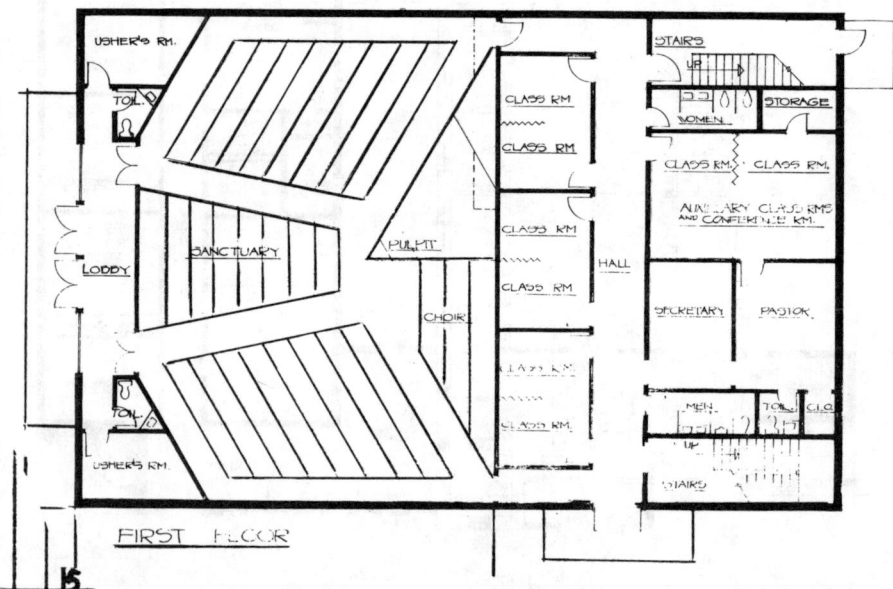

Fig. 5—**Ultra Modern church with two-story educational facility.** This structure is for the truly forward-looking pastor and congregation. Worship activities are set apart from educational activities. Concentration of educational activities in a central location is a major feature of this plan. Capacity is ca. 500–700 persons.

—Courtesy of McKISSACK & McKISSACK ARCHITECTS & ENGINEERS, INC. 330 Charlotte Avenue
Nashville, Tennessee 37201

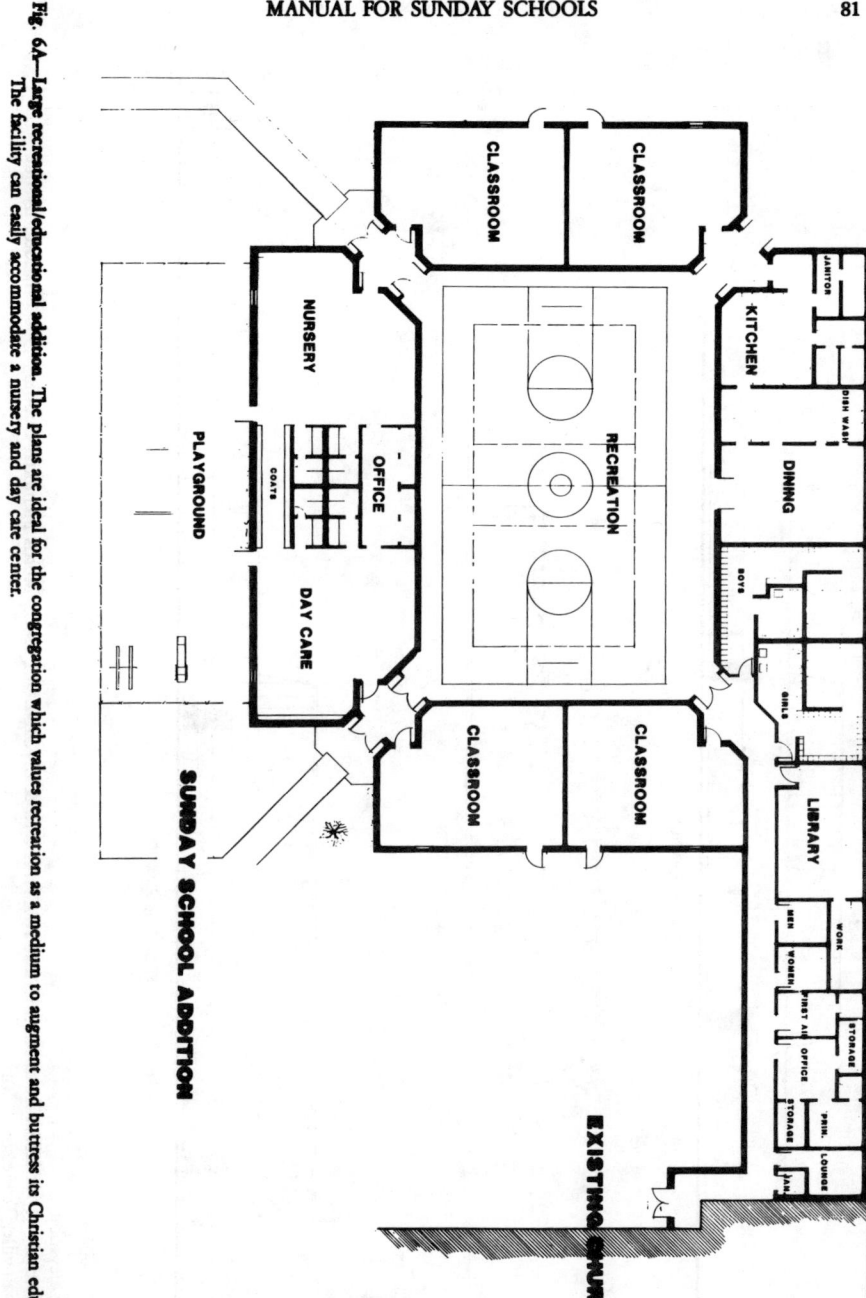

Fig. 6A—Large recreational/educational addition. The plans are ideal for the congregation which values recreation as a medium to augment and buttress its Christian education program. The facility can easily accommodate a nursery and day care center.

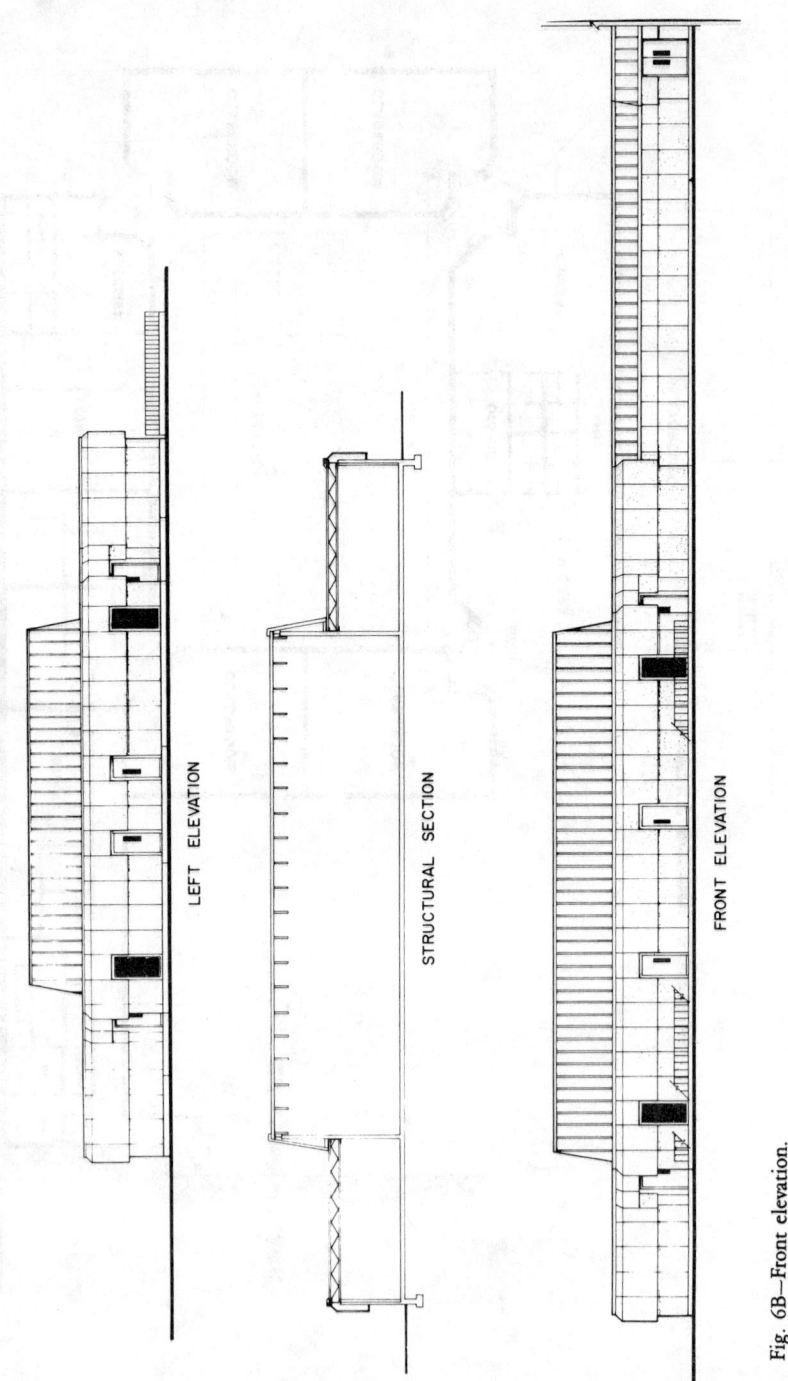

Fig. 6B—Front elevation.
Fig. 6C—Left elevation.
—Courtesy of McKISSACK & McKISSACK ARCHITECTS & ENGINEERS, INC., Morris Memorial Building, 300 Charlotte Avenue Nashville, Tennessee 37201

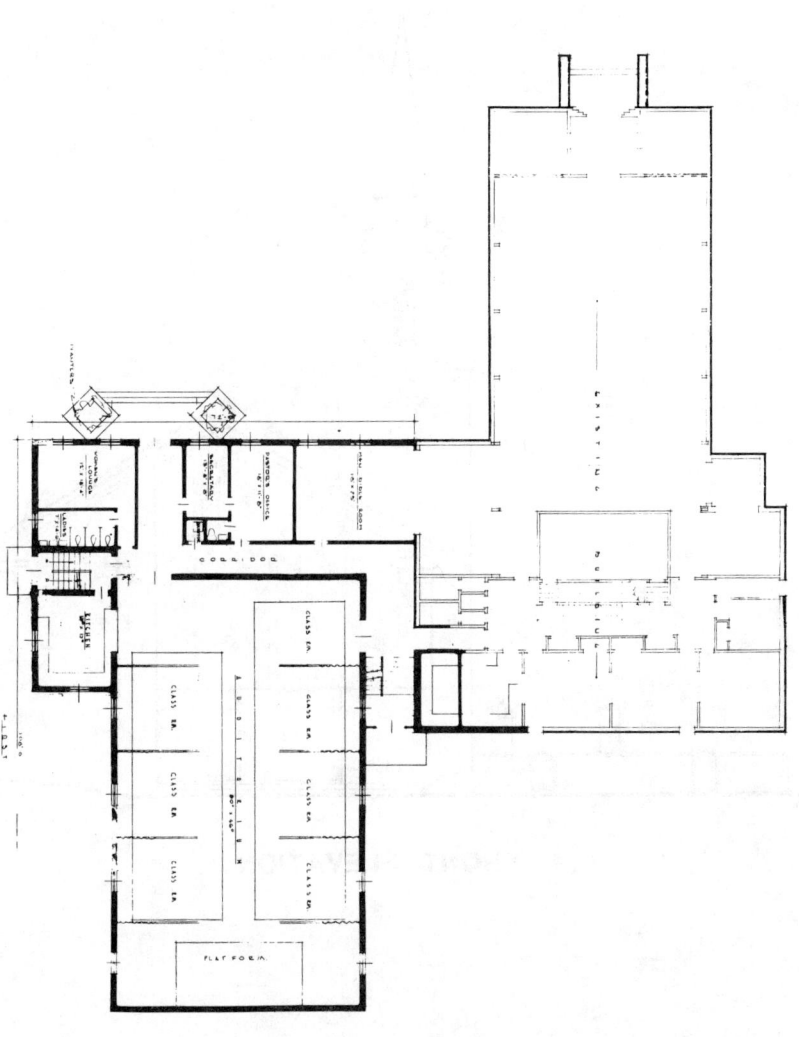

Fig. 7A—**Modern Colonial.** This facility bears the mark of distinction. Its Colonial flavor enhances the spirit of worship. Additionally, the facility is designed to accommodate large numbers (500-700) in worship and study. The entire lower level is designed for Christian education.

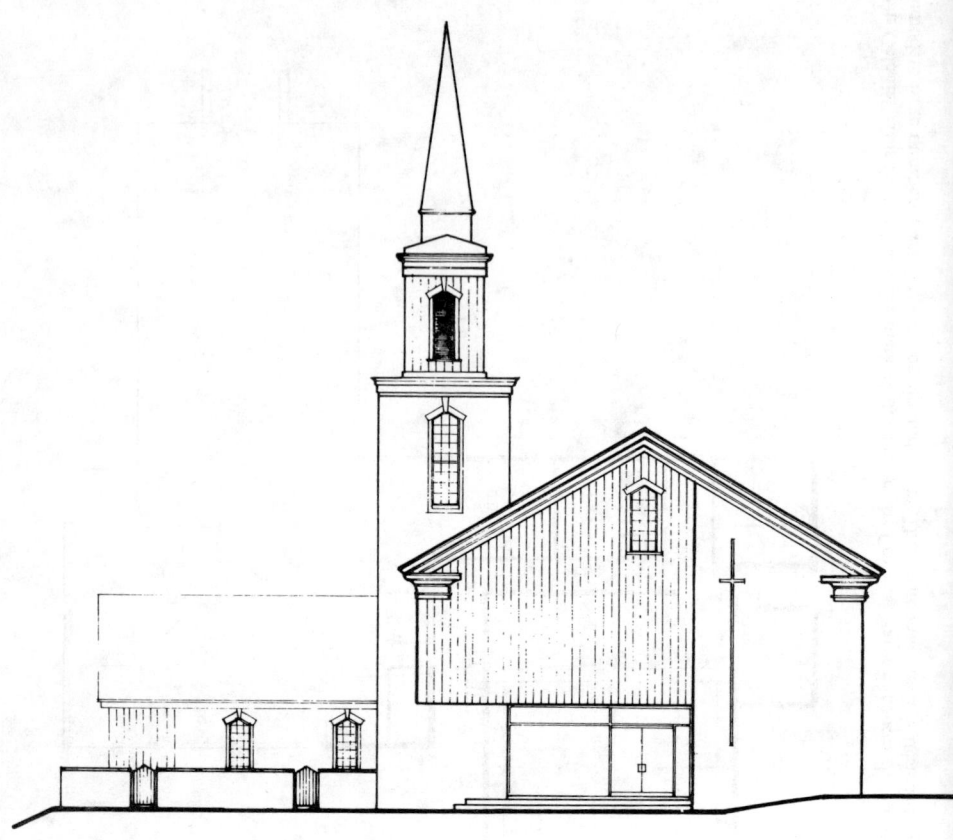

Fig. 7B—Front view Modern Colonial.

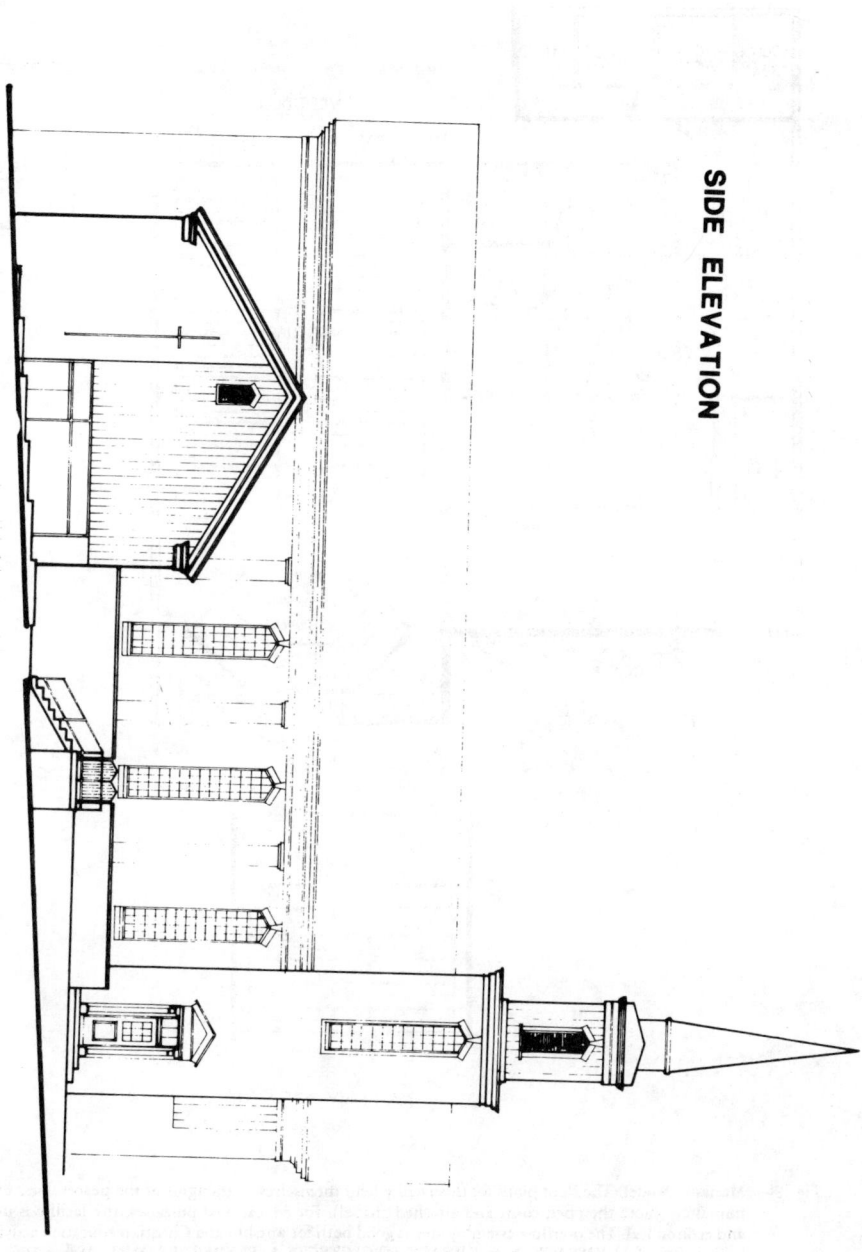

Fig. 7C—Side view Modern Colonial.
—Courtesy of McKISSACK & McKISSACK ARCHITECTS & ENGINEERS, INC., Morris Memorial Building, 330 Charlotte Avenue, Nashville, Tennessee 37201

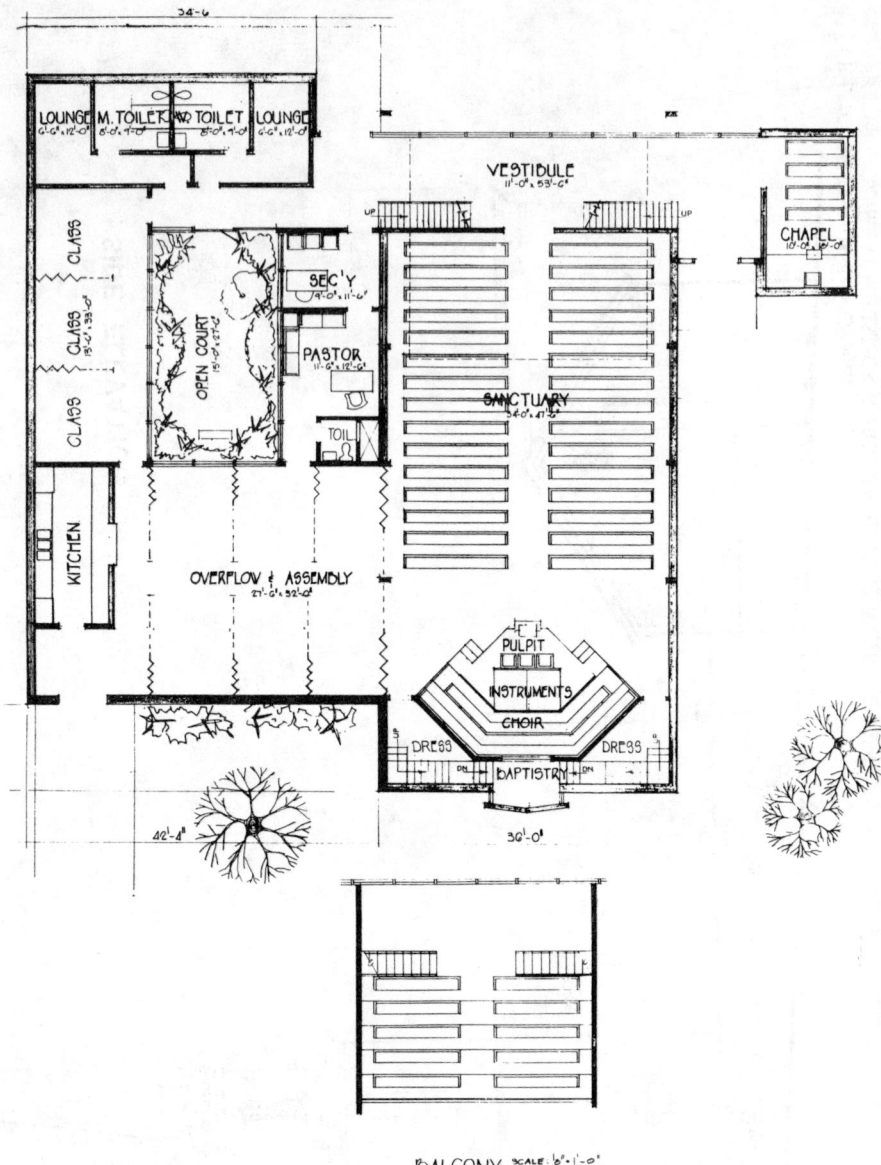

Fig. 8— **Monastic Model.** The floor plans for this facility lend themselves to thoughts of the peacefulness of the monastery (note the open court and attached chapel). For educational purposes, the facility is useful and economical. The overflow/assembly area is good both for worship and Christian education activities.
—Courtesy of McKISSACK & McKISSACK ARCHITECTS & ENGINEERS, INC., Morris Memorial Building, 330 Charlotte Avenue, Nashville, Tennessee 37201

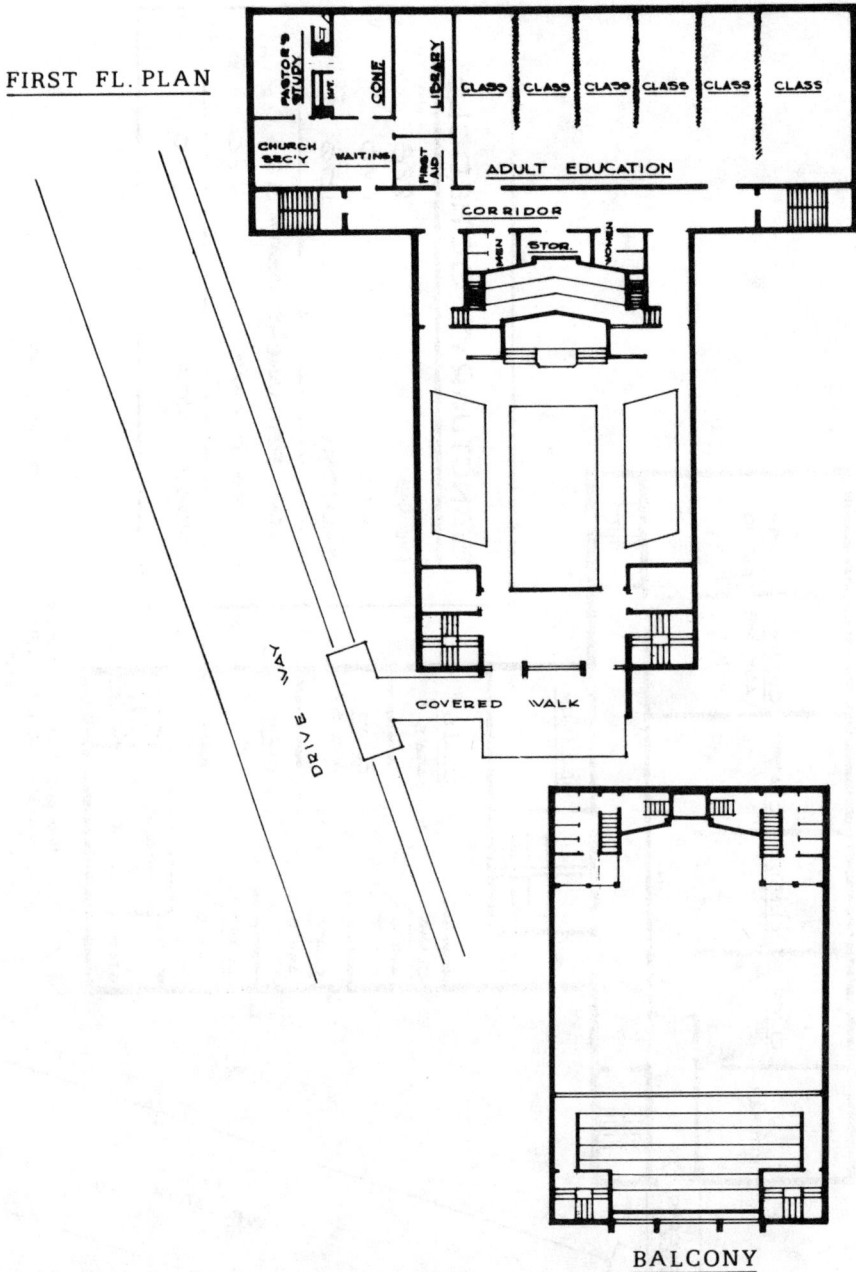

Fig. 9—**Modern "A" Frame structure.** Although the floor plans are in the form of a "T", the preponderant feature is that its external appearance is that of an "A". Christian education space is enormous inasmuch as the entire rear and lower level of the facility is designed for that purpose.

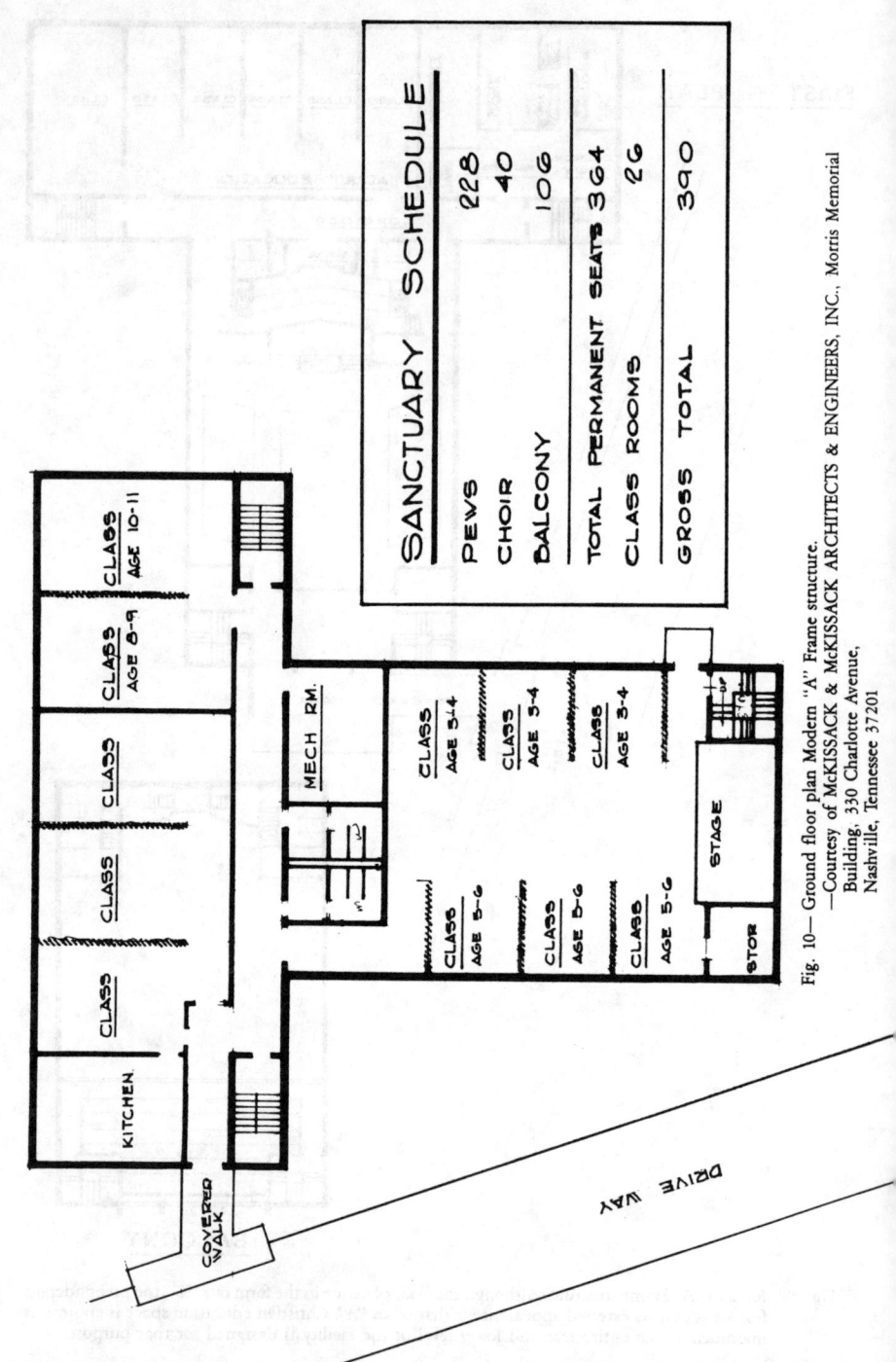

Fig. 10— Ground floor plan Modern "A" Frame structure.
—Courtesy of McKISSACK & McKISSACK ARCHITECTS & ENGINEERS, INC., Morris Memorial Building, 330 Charlotte Avenue, Nashville, Tennessee 37201

CHAPTER XI

PUBLICITY AND PROMOTION

THE effective Sunday school plans for publicizing and promoting its program. In this section of the Manual will be sugggested some methods of publicity which are effective.

Personal Contact and Invitation.

This is the best means of publicity. If the people in the Sunday school appreciate the programs, they will tell others. Also, friendly competition can be arranged among classes to publicize the work of the classes and bring other persons into the class membership.

Recognition of Visitors.

This courtesy extended to visitors will make good impressions on them, and they will go and tell others about the Sunday school. Appropriate recognition of new persons coming into the community or of those who show interest in the Sunday school will often mean new membership enrollments.

Using Special Days.

Special days in the church school year (see Section XIV of this manual) also offer great opportunity for publicity. The traditional children's programs at Christmas, Easter, Mother's Day, Children's Day, Thanksgiving etc., offer opportunity for letting parents and others know what the Sunday school is doing. Often a child learning a piece will awaken an interest in the parent; the child on program means the parent in the audience.

Special days, including Promotion Day, Decision Day, Membership Enlistment Day, and the like, with special emphasis, can help in getting the Sunday school before the people. It helps when just the words "Sunday school" reach the ears of people as often as possible. There is always room for special observances.

Sunday School Open House.

The Sunday school can publicize its program by throwing its doors open and inviting all parents, church members, and other interested persons to actually see the school at work. In this way people will become informed on what the Sunday school is all about, and they may be induced to support it better.

Sunday School Telephone Club.

People like to talk on the telephone. A group of persons in the Sunday school can form a Sunday School Telephone Club. Also, with proper information given the club, they can be in position to reach the leaders and most of the members of the Sunday school on a fairly short notice. The Telephone Club could be the medium of extending personal invitation to Sunday school functions, and for reminding officers, teachers and pupils of coming events.

Use of Newspapers.

Very often newspapers will welcome short news items about the Sunday school, especially human interest stories. A few simple rules could help here. Make the story direct and to the point; make it as short as possible; avoid excessive use of personal references; do not wait until news is "stale" before it goes to the press; do not expect too much free publicity from the newspapers.

In many daily papers special pages on Saturdays are set aside for church notices. Sunday school announcements may well be planned for this page. If possible, buy some space in the newspapers for display ads. Use those newspapers which will most effectively reach the constituency of the Sunday School.

Use of Mails.

People like to get mail-even from the Sunday school. Many cards of all types can be sent to Sunday school pupils. There are absentee reminders, invitations, convalescent and sympathy cards, attendance boosters of all types available for each age group in the Sunday school. Announcements of coming events and programs of significance can be sent cheaply through the mail.

Duplicated announcements, promotional letters, Sunday school papers, etc., may be sent through the mails as second or third class mailing matter.

Some churches use addressing machines to facilitate addressing of envelopes, cards, papers and other items for the mails. The Sunday school also could make use of these machines.

Using Mimeograph or Duplicating Materials.

There are many types of duplicators which can be used effectively in Sunday school publicity and promotion. With the use of hektograph carbon for the hektograph and the mimeoscope for the mimeograph, art work, line drawings, artistic letterings, etc., may be placed on the master copy or the stencil and duplicated. Frequently young people are interested in this type of work in the Sunday school.

The Sunday School Paper.

A very effective plan is the Sunday school paper. This paper may be produced on a mimeograph or printed at low cost. A four page weekly or monthly paper can do much to promote Sunday school work. Editorial responsibility and news reporting can be spread among the various age levels of the Sunday school. This is one activity in which all Divisions of the Sunday school can take a part.

It may be that the Young People's Division will sponsor the Sunday school paper. Or, in addition to a weekly paper of the Sunday school, the Divisions may sponsor monthlies of their own.

Distribution of Literature.

There are many leaflets, tracts, and other types of literature which can be secured for distribution by the Sunday school. A rubber stamp with appropriate message, or with just the name of the Sunday school can be used in imprinting the tracts. Bus and rail stations, stores, barber and beauty shops and other places of business offer good opportunity for distribution of such literature.

Special Programs and Social Occasions.

In addition to special emphasis days in the Sunday school (see above) there may be special programs of significance for the Sunday school. The Sunday school picnic; class, division, or school socials; parties, banquets, and the like offer great possibilities.

Campaigns.

The Sunday school can benefit from campaigns conducted. Such campaigns may be visitation campaigns, evangelistic campaigns, membership campaigns, and the like. As far as possible, these campaigns should head up in special committees responsible to the Officers' and Teachers' Meeting, In order that they may have their full effect throughout the Sunday school. On such committees there should be representation from all divisions of the Sunday school.

Use of Charts and Graphs.

Charts, graphs, posters, and the like can be used effectively for publicity. The Christian Education Advance Posters of the Sunday School Publishing Board have been found to be very helpful in stimulating attendance and in promoting Sunday school work. These posters are available at small cost from the Board.

Various types of charts and graphs can be used. A chart might be kept to show Sunday school attendance over a quarter. On the same chart, attendance might be plotted against attendance on the corresponding Sunday in the previous year, different colorings being used to denote the different years. Charts of offerings, new members, enrollments, percentage of class increase in enrollment and attendance, and many others, offer great possibilities. Much can be learned in the making of charts and posters by watching the graphic publicity representation in various civic campaigns like the United Way, and other campaigns.

Display Outdoor Advertising.

Many churches have large outside bulletin boards for making announcements of its programs. Such boards can be erected on the church grounds and used by the Sunday school to display announcements and promotion. Many other churches have small outside boards which may from time to time carry some message from the Sunday school in addition to announcements of Sunday worship service.

Register Boards and Message Boards.

These Boards, situated at some conspicuous place in the building, can call attention to Sunday school announcements and to records of attendance, offering, visitors present, etc., for a given Sunday. Banners also may be used effectively for publicity.

Pins, Buttons and Emblems.

There are many types of pins, buttons, and emblems carrying appropriate messages available for Sunday schools at comparatively small cost. Promotion Certificates, awards, and the like may be effectively used.

CHAPTER XII

THE SUNDAY SCHOOL IN ITS WIDER RELATIONSHIPS

NO Sunday school can exist entirely in and of itself. The society in which we live is interrelated. The Sunday school, therefore, enters consciously or unconsciously into a relationship with other Sunday schools and with the Christian education movement in general. The common use of literature, the acceptance of common standards, the participation in the life and work of denominational and interdenominational Sunday school organizations, are all a part of the Sunday school reaching out into wider relationships.

Subservient to Local Church Relationships.

It must be kept in mind that the Sunday school in all cases is subservient to local church relationships. Relationships with organizations outside the local church with which the Sunday school affiliates should be based on church affiliations or should have the approval and endorsement of the church as a whole.

Denominational Relationships

Sunday schools should take active part in the total life and work of Sunday school organizations in the denomination. There are many such types of affiliations which are possible.

City-wide Sunday School Organizations.

These may take the form of Baptist Sunday School Unions, Superintendent's Leagues, City-wide Sunday School Congresses or Conventions, Institutes, and other types of assemblies.

The local Sunday school should have fellowship and cooperation in the life and work of the District Sunday School Convention, Congress, or other type of district organization. Many districts carry on leadership training programs which are beneficial to all churches participating. A wide-awake program of Sunday school work at the district level provides great fellowship and can offer opportunity for stronger churches to give help and assistance to weaker ones, and help pull them up to standard in their work.

State Sunday School Organizations.

The local Sunday school should participate in the work of the Convention or Congress of the State Convention with which the church is affiliated. State-wide Sunday school work is primarily in the field of leadership training, with training courses being offered for those persons in attendance.

The Sunday school should take care in selecting persons to attend these various training enterprises. Since there is so much to be gained in leadership training it would be best to send those persons for training to these meetings who can benefit most and gain more knowledge and inspiration from them. If an adult leader is strong and a youth leader is weak, it would be better to send the youth leader than the adult for training experience.

National Sunday School Organizations.

The Congress of Christian Education is recognized as the national leadership training school in the National Baptist Convention, U. S. A., Inc. Courses of the Standard Leadership Curriculum through the Department of Christian Education of the Sunday School Publishing Board are offered. The national aspect of this meeting permits the drawing together of persons of national reputation as leaders.

This Board of the National Baptist Convention is charged with the responsibility of publishing Sunday School periodicals, hymnbooks, textbooks, religious literature, and providing other supplies and equipment for the churches and Sunday schools of the National Baptist Convention, U.S.A., Inc. It also promotes Sunday school work, and articulates the program of Christian education for the Convention. Cooperation with the Board through support of its sale of Sunday school literature and program helps does much to make possible many more services to local Sunday schools. Contributions to the Board will help strengthen its service in

Christian education to the Convention.

The National Baptist Convention, U. S. A., Inc.

By cooperating with the above mentioned denominational agencies, the local Sunday school becomes a part of the total program of work of the National Baptist Convention, U. S. A., Inc., including its program of missions, education, social service, etc.

Interdenominational and Community Relationships

The local Sunday school should take part in interdenominational and community Sunday school and Christian education work. There are some problems in the community which can best be faced cooperatively, and some projects which can best be undertaken cooperatively. Such might include attacking common problems, conducting of religious surveys, promoting attendance campaigns, creating a community "climate" favorable to Sunday school work, providing for sharing of ideas and experiences which will be of mutual benefit in leader growth and development, and the like.

Community Councils of Christian Education. Many Sunday schools will affiliate with local, city, county or area councils of Christian education. Many Sunday schools will take part in county Sunday School conventions. These organizations are worthy and deserving of the support of local Sunday schools.

State Councils of Christian Education. Sunday schools may affiliate with state councils of Christian education and with state interdenominational Sunday school conventions for inspiration and for promotion of Sunday school work.

The Division of Christian Education of the National Council of Churches. While local Sunday schools do not take membership in the NCC, participation in the organized program of Sunday school work in North America involves participation in the program of the Council. Through the NCC is provided the outlines for Sunday school lesson series, the leadership training program, the standards for Sunday school work, and many other helps for Sunday schools. The NCC sponsors the Quadrennial International Sunday School Conventions, which call together thousands of lay workers in the Sunday Schools of North America.

Relationships to other Community Organizations. The local Sunday school has a relationship and maintains an interest in all community serving organizations which are for the moral and spiritual welfare of people. Particularly is there a relationship to the public schools, because many of the pupils of the Sunday school are also pupils of the public school. The programs of these two agencies can supplement and complement each other to their mutual benefit and to the moral and spiritual development of the pupil.

Relationships to the Sunday School Publishing Board

As affiliates of the National Baptist Convention, U.S.A., Inc., and its agencies, Sunday schools should support the Sunday School Publishing Board. Assistance is available through the Sunday School Publishing Board in the following areas:

Church Administration
Sunday School Administration
Sunday School Lesson Materials
Vacation Church School Materials
  Church Supplies
    Hymn Books
    Certificates
    Church Furnishings
    Robes
    Church Record Books

Through the Department of Christian Education of the Sunday School Publishing Board help is available in the following areas:

Sunday School Administration
Leadership Education
Rural Church Work
Field Program, cooperating with State Conventions
Vacation Church School Work
Rural Church Work
Audio-Visual Education
Boys' Work
Other Areas of Service
Certification of Leadership Training Schools
Certification of Deans and Instructors
Textbooks for Course Study
Family Ministry Programs

Relationships and affiliations of the Sunday School Publishing Board include the Religious Education Association and the World's Sunday School Association, acting as the World Council of Christian Education, and the National Council of Churches. Affiliation with the Sunday School Publishing Board makes it possible for the local Sunday School to take advantage of the program of these agencies.

CHAPTER XIII

STANDARD OF EXCELLENCE FOR BAPTIST SUNDAY SCHOOLS

THE following is the Standard of Excellence for Sunday Schools as arranged by the Sunday School Publishing Board, National Baptist Convention, U. S. A., Inc.
1. Purpose and Relations
2. Standard Organization
3. Evangelism
4. Enlistment
    a. Members
    b. Workers
5. Baptist Literature
6. Worship and Music
7. Leadership Training
8. Workers' Council
9. Finance, Stewardship, Missions
10. Housing and Equipment
11. Special Days and Observances
12. Records, Reports, Promotion

EXPLANATION

I. Purpose and Relations

The Sunday school is a teaching agency of the local church. It must be under and obedient to the control of the local church. All officers and teachers nominated by the Sunday school must be approved by the church. All teaching should be in line with the missionary Baptist ideals, doctrine and program. Teachers and officers should attend the regular preaching and worship services of the church and also influence at least 60 per cent of those pupils whom they teach to attend the service regularly. The Sunday school must be a definite part of the program of the local church. The Sunday school should also participate in local, district, state, and national Sunday school organizations.

II. Standard Organization

The organization of the Sunday school should conform to or follow the plan given in this Manual in Section II and III.

A standard school must have a Cradle Roll or Nursery Department with at least one director, and observe Cradle Roll Day with some type of special service, at which time the child along with its parents must be present and introduced to the assembly. It must also have a Home Department for persons unable to attend the regular session of the Sunday school. The instruction given in the school should be based upon the curriculum materials and plans outlined and distributed by the Sunday School Publishing Board.

III. Evangelism

Seasonal and frequent special evangelistic emphasis and appeals should be made before the school by superintendents and pastor, at least quarterly. Teachers should constantly and earnestly seek the salvation and baptism of unsaved pupils, the spiritual growth of the saved in their classes, and, follow up on absentees and seek to gain new pupils for the school.

IV. Enlishtment
   a. Members
   b. Workers

A Continuing program for enlisting new members and developing workers and adequately trained leaders should be followed. Suggestions may be found in this Manual. This standard will be achieved by combining the suggestions and methods given under Evangelism and Leadership Training.

Helps in this program, may be secured from the Sunday School Publishing Board.

V. Baptist Literature

The Sunday school literature, quarterlies, lesson helps, periodicals, song books and other equipment should be secured from the Sunday School

Publishing Board, and adapted by the local Sunday school to suit each age level according to the specification cited in this Manual.

VI. Worship and Music

The worship services in the local school should be in keeping with the general or graded worship service, outlines as given in the quarterlies for each department of the school or its organized divisions or classes. Careful regard should be given to the usage of the Baptist Standard Hymnal and/or Gospel Pearl because the worship service outlines for the quarter are based upon these song books and hymnals.

VII. Training for participation and leadership in the local program of Christian education and Sunday School work is necessary.

The goal should be that the officers and teachers have at least one credit card in Leadership Training as sponsored by the Sunday School Publishing Board. Courses may be taken through district, state, and National Baptist organizations including Sunday school conventions, congresses, Woman's conventions, laymen's conventions, young people's conventions, and institutes or schools planned and sponsored through a district association or state convention, or through a local church, class or school, through community schools, or through correspondence. Each local church, community or district should operate a leadership Training Class or participate cooperatively with some other church organization in operating such a class for at least two weeks during the year. Further information and plans will be found in the Sunday School Manual and the publication, **A Manual for Leadership Education and Curriculum Guide.**

VIII. Workers' Council

The real planning for the program of the local church school is to be done in this group, which may be also known as Worker's Conference, or Officers' and Teachers' Meeting. This group consists of the pastor, officers and teachers, under the leadership of the general superintendent. A full discussion of this group and its work will be found in section VIII of this Manual. It comprises the heart of the administrative aspects of Sunday School program. The group lays the general plans, analysis, and reconstructs the existing program, sets goals, plans and objectives, as well as gives individual or specific help to workers in the local church school.

IX. Finance, Stewardship, Missions

The success of the local Sunday school is partially based on raising, using and properly disbursing the finances of the school. Section IX in this Manual gives suggestions on this subject.

Each local school should attempt to teach both by precept and example the meaning and importance of stewardship. The local Sunday school through the officers and teachers should be a good steward in using the monies of the school in ways which will give the greatest benefit to the school, students and church, all for the glory of God and the advancement of His Cause. God is the Maker, Owner, and Giver of all things. The church school must practice and teach stewardship (See Malachi 3:10; Deuteronomy 8:18; 1 Corinthians 4:2; Haggai 2:8).

Missions—the local school should participate in and support every form of missions, i.e., Home, Foreign and Educational. This should be taught to the pupils and provisions made for personal, class, division and school participation. We are members of the Missionary Baptist Church. We are working actively in the program which Jesus gave his church and disciples in "The Great Commission" (See Matthew 28:18-20).

X. Housing and Equipment

The aim of every local school should be to be sufficiently housed and equipped to adequately carry on the local program. According to the latest Sunday school standards, housing and equipment are a necessary part of the total curriculum of the local program of Christian education. Section X of the Manual will give further information.

XI. Special and Denominational Day Observances

Each school should give due emphasis to the various special and denominational days. Programs and participation should be given as suggested in this Manual. Special consideration and support should be given to the National Baptist Convention Emphasis Days as found in Section XIV of this Manual.

XII. Records, Reports, Promotion

Accurate and permanent records and reports are important in the successful and progressive administration of the local school. The importance of this phase of the educational work of the church is fully discussed and examples in Section IX of this Manual.

Publicity and promotion must be engaged in, if the local school is to be effective, wide-awake, progressive and growing. Plans and suggestions on this phase of Sunday school work are given attention in Section XI of this Manual.

Officers and teachers should make regular reports to the Sunday school on the leading activities and achievements of the school. The Sunday school, in turn, should make regular reports to the church through the local Board of Christian Education, or other designated committee.

This Standard of Excellence is arranged in 12 units, with a possible 100 per cent grade. Schools that can meet any three units in the Standard of Excellence rate 25 per cent; schools meeting six, 50 per cent; schools meeting nine, 75 per cent; schools meeting all twelve units outlined on the chart will be rated 100 per cent, or classed as Standard by the Sunday School Publishing Board of the National Baptist Convention, U. S. A., Inc.

Sunday schools should register with the Sunday School Publishing Board and begin to work toward the achievement of the Standard.

CHAPTER XIV

CALENDAR OF ACTIVITIES AND OBSERVATIONS FOR THE SUNDAY SCHOOL

THE following calendar of activities and observances is suggested for the guidance of Sunday schools in formulating their own programs. It must be remembered that there will be special emphasis days not mentioned here which will find place on the Sunday school calendar. While the suggestions are arranged in order from January to December, Sunday school workers should keep in mind the Sunday school year, October 1—September 30, in planning the Sunday school calendar.

General Observances in the Year
  New Year's Day, January 1
  Easter Sunday
  Mother's Day, second Sunday in May
  Children's Day, second Sunday in June
  Father's Day, third Sunday in June
  Thanksgiving, fourth or last Thursday in November
  Christmas, December 25

Special Local Sunday School Emphasis Days
  Promotion Day, last Sunday in September
  Religious Education Week, last Sunday in September to first Sunday in October
  Decision Day (Evangelism)

Attendance Rally Day
Sunday School Open House
Stewardship Emphasis Day
Missionary Emphasis Day
Officers and Teachers' Recognition Day
Leadership Training Periods

Other Local Emphasis
Local Sunday School Organization Meetings
District Sunday School Convention or Congress
State Sunday School Convention or Congress
National Baptist Congress of Christian Education,
 week following 3rd Sunday in June
Denominational Institutes, Workshops, Conferences
Interdenominational local, area, state, and national gatherings
Community gatherings and emphasis

Special National Baptist Convention Emphasis Days
General Promotion Day, Youth Organizations, last Sunday in January
B.T.U. Founder's Day (National B.T.U. Board), second Sunday in March
American Baptist Theological Seminary Day, third Sunday in May
Benefit Board Day, fourth Sunday in May
Sunday School Publishing Board Day, second Sunday in June
National Layman's Day (National Baptist Layman's Movement, third Sunday in June
Promotion Day (Department of Christian Education, Sunday School Publishing Board), last Sunday in September
Founder's Day, National Baptist Convention, U.S.A., Inc. Sunday nearest November 24
Foreign Missions Christmas Drive (Foreign Mission Board), December

Special Interdenominational Observances and Emphasis Days
Week of Prayer, first full week in January
Birthday of Dr. Martin Luther King, Jr., January 15
Youth Week, last Sunday in January to first Sunday in February
Race Relations Sunday, Sunday nearest February 12
Brotherhood Week, Sunday preceding February 22 through following Sunday
World Day of Prayer, first Friday in Lent

National Negro Health Week
National Family Week, first Sunday in May through the second Sunday
Rural Life Sunday, fifth Sunday after Easter
May Fellowship Day, first Friday in May
Labor Sunday, Sunday preceding Labor Day
Religious Education Week, last Sunday in September through first Sunday in October
World Communion Sunday, first Sunday in October
World Order Sunday, Sunday nearest October 24
World Community Day, first Friday in November
Universal Bible Sunday, second Sunday in December
Emancipation Proclamation Observance January 1
Birthday of Dr. Martin Luther King, Jr., January 15
Negro History Month, Month of February
Observance of Assassination of Dr. Martin Luther King, Jr., April 4

APPENDIX

APPENDIX

The History Of The National Baptist Congress of Christian Education*

by

Dr. Charles L. Dinkins

Introduction

When one looks at the National Baptist Congress of Christian Education today, one sees a vast educational enterprise, bringing together in one week of study thousands of people from hundreds of churches and other organizations throughout the constituency of the National Baptist Convention, U.S.A., Inc. These persons study in more than one hundred classes, participate in almost one hundred discussion groups, and involve themselves in nine special project areas of study and discussion. They gain exposure to the top people in Christian education in the Convention, and to trends in Christian education both inside and outside of the denomination. These persons are inspired, trained, encouraged, and they become important links in the chain of effort to provide a channel through which the National Baptist Convention seeks to improve Christian education in its member churches through Sunday schools, Baptist Training Unions, and other church educational activities.

The influence of the Congress, however, is not limited to its one-week activity in the year. What happens in the week between the third and fourth Sundays in June is the result of year-round effort in planning, managing and evaluating on the part of hundreds of people who volunteer their time and effort for the purpose. The Congress operates without fulltime professional staff, and depends for its leadership, from officers to faculty to committee members, upon people who give unselfishly of their service, receiving only modest "honoraria" for their effort. But their leadership and service make possible a strong visibility for Christian education in the largest black religious organization in the world. The Congress serves as a model for states, districts, and other units of Baptist organization and activity. The themes developed in the Congress are used throughout the denomination, providing cohesion and direction for a national effort, and articulation for national emphases and thrusts in Christian education.

*Written to commemorate the 75th year anniversary of the National Baptist Congress of Christian Education in 1980.

The Congress is the educational arm of the National Baptist Convention, U.S.A., Inc. The Congress operates its own program, but reports to and receives approval for its plans from the Convention, and the Convention's Board of Directors, and President. The Congress functions on the basis of its own constitution which defines its purpose, its constituency, its pattern of organization, its officers and their functions, and its relation to the parent Convention and the Convention's agencies. The Congress is not an independent unit. It depends for its educational program on the Sunday School Publishing Board and the National Baptist Training Union Board, each of which is charged by the Convention with year-round responsibility for planning and implementing Christian education activity in the Convention through the production of curriculum materials and supportive programs, through leader and worker development and organizational design.

The Congress functions through a Board of Directors which is amenable to the Convention, and officers whose election is subject to review and approval by the Convention and its Board of Directors. These officers are elected by the "messengers" who attend the congress. The officers in turn recommend the leadership for its functional units—educational, management and service. These leaders in turn become a part of the executive administration of the Congress. Under these persons, who form the Executive Committee of the Congress, there serve hundreds of faculty persons, discussion leaders, project directors, supervisors, coordinators, committee members, and others, each contributing to the uniqueness of the Congress as it carries out its mission.

The present pattern of Congress organization and activity has been seventy-five years in the making. During this time the Congress has been responsive to changes inside and outside its organization which in turn have influenced the development of the Congress and its activities. In this article we will note some of these.

The history of seventy-five years cannot effectively be capsuled into a few short pages, so the effort will be made here to present an overview of what has developed in these seventy-five years, and the major trends and movements which have affected that development and shaped the course of Congress activity. The material is taken from printed documents, minutes, programs, evaluations, news articles and other sources. But much of it is also drawn out of an association with the Congress of more than thirty-five years, and personal relations and involvements with many of the principal characters in its development. Some of the persons in the latter category are those who were involved in Congress activity as far back as 1916. Because the Congress has been served by so many persons who have contributed to its growth and development, it will not be possible to give appropriate recognition to them. So, such names as appear must be seen as representatives of the services of their contemporaries at the time.

The presentation is over-simplified for it is not possible to trace in detail all of the influences inside and outside the Congress which have affected it. It is not possible to deal with the social context which has affected the development of Black Church educational activity in general, and Baptist activities specifically. It is not possible in these few pages to deal with the influence of the Christian education enterprise generally on the Congress or to trace in detail the events in the convention, historical and political, which have affected the Congress. No statistical information on enrollments or finances is included. No effort has been made to trace the effects of institutions like schools, colleges, or missionary activity sponsored by black and white groups. What is presented here is at best an introduction to the trends, the ideas, the programs, and the people who have helped shape the Congress into what it is today.

Background to 1915

In the days of slavery there were those who believed that black people should be subjects for evangelization into the Christian religion. They believed that slaves had souls that should be saved, even though their bodies were in bondage. In many places the efforts to evangelize black people were also accompanied by efforts to teach them. In fact, the early efforts at teaching black people to read and write were to enable them to be better Christians, more docile, and therefore better slaves. The early textbook was the Bible; early teachers were often women who saw this effort as an extension of their Christian witness and service. As blacks learned to read the Bible, however, they came to learn its essential message of freedom. They often formed their own churches, heard their own preachers, developed their own associations and missionary programs. The first Sunday school in America was started by a black woman. As early as the 1820s blacks were sending missionaries to Africa to spread the Christian gospel among the people.

With emancipation from slavery came a renewed effort by white denominations, as well as blacks themselves, to bring education and evangelism to the newly freed persons. White denominations, as well as blacks who had secured some education and training, engaged in a great missionary effort to establish schools and churches to serve the needs of the freed persons. Baptists of the north and south, who had split in 1845 over the question of slavery, shared in this effort. The result was schools and churches throughout the south, with missionaries serving as teachers and leaders. As black people became trained, they in turn trained others and developed their own network of institutions, organizations, programs and activities.

In 1880 the call came to organize the first Convention among Colored Baptists. The National Baptist Convention dates its origin at that time. In 1895 in a merger with other groups the name National Baptist Convention was adopted. At that time the Convention sponsored a Home Mission and a Foreign Mission Board, but the people depended on northern and southern Baptist agencies for educational materials, books, and literature to serve their needs. Efforts to include qualified black scholars on the staffs preparing these materials were rebuffed by the leaders of the respective white groups. The materials that blacks were using was the same as that being used by whites, but with covers identifying the editions used by black churches. As black theologians and writers developed, the cry went up that these qualified persons should share in the preparation of material to be used not only in black Baptist churches, but in Baptist churches in general. In the National Baptist Convention the cry went up against literature with "white guts and black backs." In response to this cry, Dr. R. H. Boyd of Texas, who at the time was Secretary of the Home Mission Board of the Convention, organized the National Baptist Publishing Board, and became its Secretary. He moved both Boards to Nashville, Tennessee, which by this time had become a center for religious publishing for other denominations. Soon afterwards, Dr. E. W. D. Isaac, Sr., who was secretary of the Baptist Young People's Union Board, moved that Board's headquarters from Texas to Nashville. Both Boards embarked upon programs to produce literature for the churches.

These events, however, cannot be isolated from other developments which were taking place in Christian eduction. The International Sunday School Convention, the International Society of Christian Endeavor, the American Sunday School Union, and the development of International Sunday School Union, and the development of International Sunday School Lessons, are all a part of the history of this period. As black schools and colleges produced graduates, these persons were indoctrinated with their own self-awareness. The schools and colleges provided a platform for black leaders to speak and for young minds to be impressed. As the graduates left the schools they became the backbone of the churches which were developing. Preachers and teachers, and some professionals, gave strong leadership also in district, state, and national conventions. Booker T. Washington was a speaker in sessions of the National Baptist Convention until his death in 1915. Strong laymen supported missionary and educational activities, and alongside ministers helped establish institutions to carry out these activities.

But the training programs sponsored by the northern and southern conventions continued. The representatives of these groups presented and promoted use of the materials produced by their sponsors. It became apparent that if black Baptists were to effectively meet this challenge they would have to develop their own programs for extending the use of their materials, and for training people in how to develop Sunday schools, Young People's Unions, and other such organizations in their churches. Northern and Southern Baptist Conventions developed assemblies for training and inspiring the workers who would use their programs and materials.

In 1905 the National Baptist Convention adopted the idea of a Chautauqua through which to promote its educational programs and materials. A call went out for the churches to send messengers to Nashville, Tennessee, in 1906 for the first national Sunday and B.Y.P.U. Chautauqua, to be sponsored by the National Baptist Publishing Board and the National Baptist Young People's Union Board. The moving spirit behind the effort was Dr. Richard Henry Boyd, Corresponding Secretary of the National Baptist Publishing Board. Newspaper accounts of early sessions of the Congress are found in the files of **The National Baptist Union (Review).**

In the second session of the Congress, held in New Orleans in 1907, Dr. L. S. Simon of Louisiana welcomed the delegates, stating that "there are nearly twice as many delegates as were in Nashville last year." In a session of the Convention at which there was a celebration of the 50th anniversary of the Emancipation Proclamation, Rev. W. H. Moses, president of Guadalupe College, said, "This man (Dr. R. H. Boyd) with the assistance of his godly son (Dr. Henry Allen Boyd), who is the power behind the throne, has organized the great Negro Baptist Sunday School Congress which meets annually in different sections of the United States of America, for inspiration and high grade instruction in Sunday school methods."

Dr. T. B. Boyd, III and Dr. Samuel L. Johnson, officials of the National Baptist Publishing Board, furnished these quotations from the files of **The National Baptist Union Review.** In the issue of March 16, 1918, the following statement is carried: "Thirteen years ago in June, the first session of the Sunday School Congress was held. When the announcement went forth that the movement had been launched for the benefit of the Sunday School forces and the B.Y.P.U. workers, it was hailed with joy and delight. Strong editorials by the leading denominational editors appeared in papers throughout the country. Secular journals declared it was beyond measure the proper time, and that the meeting was calculated to do what no other had done. It would, in other words, be the little leaven in the loaf. So, in June, 1906, the movement was launched at Nashville, Tennessee. In 1907, it met in New Orleans, Louisiana; in 1908, Jacksonville, Florida; in 1909, Nashville, Tennessee; in 1910, Atlanta, Georgia; in 1911, Meridian, Mississippi; in 1912, Tuskegee, Alabama; in 1913, Muskogee, Oklahoma; in 1914, Beaumont, Texas; in 1915, Birmingham, Alabama; in 1916, Vicksburg, Mississippi; in 1917, Nashville, Tennessee; and this year (1918), Alexandria, Louisiana."

The files of the **Union Review,** March 16, 1918, also list the departments of the Congress divided into the areas of Sunday School work, B.Y.P.U. work, and special features. Under the heading of Sunday School work, there were .Superintendent', the Intermediates', the Advanced Teachers', the Cradle Roll and Infants', the Home Extension, the Boy Cadets', and the Sunday School Missionary Departments. For the B.Y.P.U. there were the Christian Culture Course, the Reading Course and the Missionary Departments. Special features included the Sociological and Industrial Education Department, providing information for making the best use of Publishing Board literature, and demonstrating methods in Sunday School work; the Congress parade, Metoka and Galeda Night, and the Model Sunday School, "at the hour designated by the host church."

The events which led to the separation of the Convention into two groups in 1915 were felt in the Congress. Some leaders on both sides of the separation sounded the alarm that the parting of the ways would result in irreparable harm to the entire Baptist constituency. The separation was especially keen in the Congress, where there was loss in dedicated and talented workers from both sides. Nevertheless, the two groups pulled their respective supporters together, and after some adjustment continued their efforts in Christian education.

From 1916 to 1930

At the time of the separation of the Sunday School Congress, which followed in the wake of the separation of the National Baptist Convention into two groups, the pattern of Congress activity was established. In 1915 the Home Mission Board and the National Baptist Publishing Board withdrew from the parent body, and with their supporters organized the National Baptist Convention of America. The National B.Y.P.U. Board remained with the National Baptist Convention of the United States of America, later to become known as "the incorporated Convention." Following the withdrawal of the National Baptist Publishing Board, the National Baptist Convention, U.S.A., formed the Sunday School Publishing Board to carry out responsibilities which had previously been those of the National Baptist Publishing Board. The Convention, now without a Congress, since the Sunday School Congress was related to the National Baptist Publishing Board, issued a call to the churches remaining in the Convention, to send representatives of their Sunday schools and B.Y.P.U's to a meeting in Memphis, Tennessee, in 1916. At this meeting a constitution was developed, and the National Sunday School and B.Y.P.U. Congress was organized. Dr. D. W. Cannon was elected President. Dr. W. H. Jernagin was elected Vice President, Dr. E. W. D. Isaac, Sr., was elected Director General. Miss Lucie E. Campbell was elected Music Director. From this beginning in 1916 we will trace the developments to the present.

Although the Congress had its own officers, the real control of the Congress rested in the Boards which sponsored it. The Congress afforded the opportunity for these Boards to display their materials, and to train persons in the use of the materials and in organizing Sunday schools and Baptist Young People's Unions in the churches. To insure this relation the positions of Director General and Associate Director General of the Congress were the Corresponding Secretaries of the two sponsoring Boards, with the senior Secretary being the Director General, and the junior Secretary being Associate Director General. Thus Dr. E. W. D. Isaac, Sr. became the first Director General. In 1920, with the election of Dr. A. M. Townsend as Secretary of the Sunday School Publishing Board, he became the Associate Director General of the Congress. Upon the death of Dr. E. W. D. Isaac, Sr., Dr. Townsend became Director General of the Congress. Dr. E. W. D. Isaac, Jr., who succeeded his father as Secretary of the National B.Y.P.U. Board, became Associate Director General. In 1926, following the death of Dr. D. W. Cannon, Dr. W. H. Jernagin was elected President of the Congress. Dr. O. Clay Maxwell was elected Vice President.

The relationship of the Congress to the Boards was firmly established. The Congress was operated in effect as arms of the sponsoring Boards. The Congress program continued the singing, parades, displays, demonstrations, model Sunday schools and B.Y.P.U.'s and other features. E. W. D. Isaac, Jr. and Lucie E. Campbell wrote songs for the Congress and published song books which became widely used throughout the denomination. These books, together with the Baptist Standard Hymnal, published by the Sunday School Publishing Board, set the standard for church music throughout the denomination. Gospel Pearls, Spirituals Triumphant, Inspirational Melodies, and other song books were promoted in the Congress.

The new leadership of the Congress began to pull together a program of activity so that a curriculum for the Congress began to emerge. Dr.

S. N. Vass had for many years served on the staff of the American Baptist Publication Society, conducting training programs in churches and districts across the nation. He was an outstanding leader, long in service, and respected throughout the Negro Baptist family. Dr. Vass was invited to come to the Sunday School Publishing Board as Director of Christian Education, with major responsibility for developing the program to train teachers and leaders in Sunday school methods. He developed what became known as the Vass Leadership Curriculum. The curriculum for leadership training was in three books written by him and published by the Sunday School Publishing Board. The titles of the Books were, **The Study of the Old Testament, The Study of the New Testament,** and **Principles and Methods of Religious Education.** The latter book was divided into three sections, "The Pupil Learning," "The Teacher Teaching," and "The School Functioning." In addition, the Sunday School Publishing Board produced books on Baptist Doctrine, Church Manuals, and Guides for Sunday Schools, Missionary Societies and other organizations in the Church. The National B.Y.P.U. Board produced manuals and guides for young people's organizations and the Christian Culture course. These publications were widely promoted throughout the Congress. Other books were written by Congress workers during this period. It was the practice to teach a class, write the material for the class, and sell it.

The pattern for the Congress curriculum was developed in the two Boards, and given to the Congress by the Boards. Leadership positions in the Congress were given to persons who came to the attention of the Boards, and who were considered loyal to the Boards and their leadership. Both the Sunday School Publishing Board and the National B. Y. P. U. Board retained field workers to move about through the constituency and promote the use of the products of the Boards. The efforts of the Sunday School Publishing Board also included use of these field workers in campaigns to pay off the indebtedness on the Morris Memorial Building, home of the Sunday School Publishing Board, in Nashville. The National Baptist Convention issued bonds for this purpose, and field workers promoted campaigns to raise the money to retire bonds by asking people in the churches to contribute quarters and to purchase the materials of the Boards.

In supporting the work of the Boards and the Congress people were also supporting the Convention. The campaign to pay the debt of the Publishing House resulted in both contributions and profits. It further provided a means of identifying the national affiliations of churches by where they bought their Sunday school materials, since most churches that bought literature did not "represent" in the Convention, but contributed through campaigns and the profits of the Boards. These profits were appropriated for the work of the Convention. Naturally, the Boards recommended for service in the Congress those persons who contributed to the work of the Boards.

From 1930 to 1943

In the early 1930s Dr. Marshall A. Talley came to the Sunday School Publishing Board as Secretary of the Christian Education Department, succeeding Dr. S. N. Vass. Dr. Talley found the Board using the Vass Leadership Curriculum as the basis for its training programs. At the same time the Sunday School Publishing Board was basing its lesson materials on the Uniform Lessons Series. The production of these lessons, begun in 1872, was coordinated through the International Council of Religious Education. Dr. Talley saw his task as that of tying the educational program of the Sunday School Publishing Board to the interdenominational effort developed through the International Council. He also was influenced by the pattern of the program of the International Sunday School Association, which was also coordinated by the International Council, although the Sunday School Association was an independent organization. In the International Council of Religious Education several major denominations were represented, not only for the production of curriculum materials, but for the development of programs in children's work, youth work, adult work, leadership education, missionary education, and other areas of Christian education activity. Working committees of the Council included representatives of various denominations. Materials developed through the Council were often produced cooperatively through the Cooperative Publishing Association, in which several denominations shared membership and shared responsibility for producing leadership and program texts and materials.

Among these dominations were both the Southern and Northern Baptists. The Southern Baptists participated in the development of the Uniform Sunday School lessons and other curriculum materials, but did not participate in the other programs of the International Council. On the other hand, the Northern Baptists participated both in the Lessons Committees and in other programs of the Council, based on their denominational membership in the Council. At the same time, both these Baptist denominations were conducting missionary and educational activities among Negro Baptist churches. The Southern Baptists appointed field workers and "teacher-Missionaries." The Northern Baptists sponsored Eduational Centers in metropolitan areas, serving the needs of those churches. Southern Baptists had their own training program, including courses in Baptist Training Union work. The Northern Baptists used the training programs developed through the International Council of Religious Education. The programs of both denominations reached into churches of the National Baptist Convention which were using literature produced by the Sunday School Publishing Board. And, the missionaries encouraged use of the materials produced by the agencies which sponsored them and paid their salaries.

Meanwhile, both the Sunday School Publishing Board and the National B.Y.P.U., Board developed Standards of Excellence for Sunday Schools and Baptist Young People's Unions respectively. These standards were widely publicized, and were often found in local churches hanging on the walls as constant reminders to the leaders in these respective church organizations. The standards of excellence, along with the literature and supportive administrative and record books, set the pattern for Christian education in the churches.

By this time the pattern for the organization of the Congress work was established. Classes in Sunday School work, known as the Sunday School Division, were held in the mornings, directed by Dr. Talley; classes in B.Y.P.U., work, known as the B.Y.P.U., Division, were held in the afternoons, directed by Dr. F. L. Sanders. A Pastor's Seminar developed programs which were of interest to ministers and brought before them some of the outstanding preachers of the denomination. As Secretary of the Christian Education Department of the Sunday School Publishing Board, Dr. Talley represented the Board and thus the Convention's constituency in matters relating to educational program.

The International Council developed the Standard Leadership Curriculum as an interdenominational training program for church workers. This was important at the time because of the influence of Councils of Churches and Councils of Religious Education which were organized across denominational lines in many states and communities. The implementation of a common training program meant that persons taking courses in community leadership training schools could get credits through their own denominational training programs; it also meant that these denominations could share the responsibility for producing the basic texts and leadership guides which would serve the cooperating denominations. Linking the Sunday School Publishing Board's training program to the International Council through the adoption of the Standard Leadership Curriculum meant that the Board, and consequently the Congress and the Convention, would have access to the mainstream of Christian education, and participate in a system which was larger than that of the denomination itself. Participation in the Standard Leadership Curriculum thus brought textbooks, leadership education materials, and the work of top leaders in the field of Christian Education to the constituency of the Convention and Congress, and at the same time afforded opportunity for input into the work and effort of the International Council. Since Dr. Talley sat in the position of Dean of the Congress as well as Secretary of Christian Education of the Sunday School Publishing Board, the position of the Congress in relation to the interdenominational effort was also established. As Secretary of Religious Education he participated in the work of the International Council of Religious Education and the International Sunday School Association, and coordinated the use of the Standard Leadership Curriculum throughout the constituency of the Convention. As Dean of the congress he was able to use this curriculum as the basis for the Congress' educational effort, and build support for it throughout the constituency of the Convention.

Dr. Talley made another significant contribution to the work of the Congress. In 1932, he presented the idea of developing Four-year themes for the Congress and was given the responsibility for working out these themes. The themes, recommended by the Dean, set the tone for the Congress, its public addresses, and offered an opportunity for the Dean to present a "keynote address" to introduce the theme in each Congress session. The pattern was still Sunday School Division classes in the mornings, followed by a General Assembly. The B. Y. P. U., Division met in the afternoons. Public sessions were held at night.

One aspect of the Standard Leadership Curriculum program was recognition of progress through the issuance of First, Second and Third Certificates of Progress. Dr. Talley carried this program a step further by tying the curriculum to a Congress program to produce "graduates." Thus, in 1939, the first "graduating class" of the Congress was produced in a session at Tulsa, Oklahoma. One of the members of this first class was Mrs. Willa A. Townsend, wife of Dr. A. M. Townsend. Giving the Address to the class was Rev. A. McEwen Williams, now Associate Dean of the Congress.

In another effort to develop the Congress in the image of a school, Dr. Talley encouraged the organization of the Faculty Club. Dr. L. R. Mitchell of Chicago, Illinois, was chosen as President of this group. In those days, congress faculty members received an honorarium of $10.00 for their services when the income of the Congress warranted it.

In the meantime, the Congress as a structured organization was following the leadership of its president, Dr. W. H. Jernagin. Dr. Jernagin's position as a leader was not only felt in the Congress itself, but also in his relations with organizations and agencies external to the Congress. Following Dr. Jernagin's interests, the Congress became the Convention's arm in dealing with Boy Scouts, the American Bible Society, the Chaplaincy Corps the Youth Committee of the Baptist World Alliance, the

Fraternal Council of Churches, and other groups. Dr. Jernagin was hailed as the leader of the nation's young people, and stepped into the vacuum in these areas which had been created because of the interest of the leaders of the Convention in other areas of activity. The Congress paid the representation fees and sponsored the participation of Dr. Jernagin in the work of these agencies. At the same time it provided an entree for these agencies into the constituency of the Convention.

In the meantime, the finances of the Congress were being augmented by support from the Sunday School Publishing Board, and to a limited degree by the B. Y. P. U., Board. Theoretically, any "profits" from the operation of the Congress were to be shared by the Boards. In a similar manner, any "deficits" in the Congress would be made up for by the Boards. "Profits" in the Congress would enable the Boards to carry out missionary work. But, more and more the Boards were being asked to absorb the cost overruns of the Congress. And, this was at a time when the Sunday School Publishing Board was also assuming responsibility for the Convention's involvement in the American Baptist Theological Seminary, the National Baptist Missionary Training School, the retirement of the Convention's bonded indebtedness, in addition to insuring its own operations. In this period of time were two major developments which took place concurrently.

First, after the first Four-Year Program developed by Dr. Talley, President Jernagin appointed a commission on Four-Year Program to develop the next themes. The effect was some decrease in the visibility of the Dean as the organizer of the educational work of the Congress. The role of the Dean became one of a recommender, subject to acceptance by a Commission, and presented as the Commission's work through the President of the Congress. This put the President of the Congress in the position of being the person to articulate the Four-Year program as well as provide leadership in other areas of Congress activity. Although the Dean of the Congress continued to give the "Keynote Address," it sounded more and more a reflection of the work of the Commission than it reflected the work and personality of the Dean. In controversy over the position of the Dean in relation to the Congress Four Year Program, Dr. Talley submitted his resignation as Dean of the Congress. This resignation was accepted by the President of the Congress, but was rejected by the Director General of the Congress, who was also Secretary of the Sunday School Publishing Board. The ground for the rejection was that since Dr. Talley was serving as Secretary of Christian Education of the Sunday School Publishing Board, he could not resign one position without resigning the other. And that since the Boards assumed responsibility for the finances of the Congress, the Dean was in his position by appointment as a part of his activities for the Sunday School Publishing Board and the denomination. The point was further made that the basic responsibility of the Dean was to the Board which paid his salary on a full-time basis, and that he received only an "honorarium" for his service to the Congress.

Second, the involvement of President Jernagin in the various agencies where he represented the Congress meant that the financial resources of the Congress were used to underwrite this activity. Increasing costs for these activities put a strain on Congress resources which might be available for other purposes. Since the Boards were to share "profits" they also were to share "deficits." At the time the Sunday School Publishing Board was carrying the financial responsibility for several Convention activities and institutions. As the only agency producing net income which could be available for Convention work, it was being asked to do more and more things for the Convention, and assume more responsibilities. The Sunday School Publishing Board considered subsidy for the Congress as equitable in terms of its contributions to religious education in the denomination, but not in terms of underwriting the participation of the Congress in agencies outside the Convention.

The result of these developments was a new constitution adopted in 1943, which spelled out relations between the Congress and the Boards, and which make the Congress independent of the Boards. Membership in the Congress was defined. The new constitution stated that the six Boards of the Convention should be the "participating Boards" of the Congress (Article VI), and that these Boards should share in the profits of the Congress. The Boards were also to share the deficits, or to be deprived of profits until their proportionate share of deficits had been met. This Constitution was approved by the National Baptist Convention. But the net effect since its adoption is that the Congress has operated with fiscal independence from the Boards of the Convention.

Dr. Talley resigned his position as Dean of the Congress, and subsequently resigned as Director of Christian Education for the Sunday School Publishing Board. By 1943 Dr. A. Franklin Fisher had succeeded Dr. Talley in the position of Dean of the Congress. Dr. Talley was succeeded in the Sunday School Publishing Board by Dr. Jesse Jai McNeil, then in 1943 by Charles L. Dinkins. Upon the adoption of the new Constitution, Dr. E. W. D. Isaac, Jr., became Director General of the Congress, and Dr. E. C. Estell, who held no formal relationship to any of the Convention Boards, was elected Associate Director General. Thus by the end of 1943 the independence of the Congress from the Boards had been established. An interesting sidelight, however, is that the mother of A. Franklin Fisher, Dean of the Congress, and the grandmother of Charles L. Dinkins, Secretary of Christian Education in the Sunday School

Publishing Board, were sisters, so that "cousins" were in positions in the Congress and the Board where they could influence the developments to come.

Another interesting sidelight is that during the controversy between the Congress and the Sunday School Publishing Board, Dr. Jernagin and Dr. Townsend remained fast personal friends and professional associates. On Dr. Jernagin's trips to Nashville, he stayed in Dr. Townsend's home. On Dr. Townsend's trips to Washington, he stayed in Dr. Jernagin's home. Their disagreements on principles and programs had no adverse effect on their personal relationships.

From 1943 to 1950

The new constitution which spelled out the independence of the Congress and the Boards from each other also meant freedom for the Congress to develop its own program of activities, and for the Sunday School Publishing Board and the National B.Y.P.U., Board to do the same. But it also meant that the Congress and the Boards could serve in a "check and balance" relationship with each other. The visibility of the Congress, a one-week-in-the-year Leadership Training School, operating with volunteer leadership, was unique in every respect. But this visibility was complemented by the ongoing servicing of a year-round denominational effort in leadership training. The Congress had no resources to operate as an agency for the denomination. The International Council of Religious Education related to its member denominations through official Boards of Christian Education and Publishing Houses. On the other hand, the Sunday School Publishing Board had no organization through which to present itself and its programs to its constituency. Thus began a new era in relationships between the Congress and the Boards, which in turn served to strengthen the overall denominational effort in Christian education.

An important development during this period came with the election of Mrs. Bessie S. Estell in 1944 as Secretary of the Congress. This was the first time that a Secretary for the Congress had been elected without participation by the Boards. It helped spell independence for the Congress, but it also brought into the Congress a voice of conciliation which kept before the Congress its mission and role for service.

During the period of 1943-50 there were some other developments in the Congress. In response to the call for servicing the needs of ministers wives as a special group, the Ministers Wives Division of the Congress was established. The moving spirit behind this development was Dr. Mary

O. Ross, who now serves as President of the Women's Convention, Auxiliary to the National Baptist Convention, U.S.A., Inc. There was also a call for greater opportunity for expression for young people who attended the Congress. This led to the establishment of Youth Rally, with Mrs. Pauline J. Campbell as the moving spirit behind the development. Each of these persons brought a continuing interest in their respective areas which saw the programs firmly established as important units in the Congress effort.

In the meantime there was developing in the Sunday School Publishing Board an emphasis on expanding the concept of Christian education from leadership education to include the development of educational programs for the entire church. In this period the Sunday School Publishing Board expanded its program to include programs in Missionary Education, Vacation Bible School Work, Rural Church Work, Children's Work, Field Work, and Boy's Work, adding professional staff persons to develop these respective areas. One aspect of the program was to secure the appointment of full-time Directors of Christian Education in State Conventions affiliated with the National Baptist Convention, with the Sunday School Publishing Board underwriting one-third of the salary of such persons. This program also extended to appointments of Directors of Rural Church work in various states. This was possible because the mortgage on the Morris Memorial Building was burned in 1942.

In the meantime, the departure of Dr. Talley from the Congress and the Sunday School Publishing Board meant that the Congress was without representation on the program committees of the International Council of Religious Education. The effect was felt mostly in relation to the Leadership Education committee of the Council, which had responsibility for developing and serving the needs of the Standard Leadership Curriculum. The appointments to the ICRE committee were made by the Sunday School Publishing Board, which was the agency of the Convention holding membership in the Council. The ICRE itself was independent in its relation to other interdenominational agencies. The merger into the National Council of the Churches of Christ in the U.S.A., In which the ICRE became the Division of Christian Education of the National Council, did not take place until 1950.

Appointments were made by the Sunday School Publishing Board to the Children's Work Committee, the Youth Work Committee, the Adult Work Committee, the Leadership Education Committee, the Uniform Lessons Committee, and other committees of the ICRE. The Sunday School Publishing Board arranged for the appointment of the Dean of the Congress as a member of the Leadership Education committee of the ICRE, to serve on this committee alongside the Secretary of Christian

Education of the Board. Through this exposure to developments in the field of Christian education the Congress and the Board found a common ground to address some of the problems that were emerging.

1. Accrediting the Congress.

The Congress granted course cards to persons who completed eight hours of work in classes during the congress sessions. The course cards for classes in the Sunday School Division came from the Sunday School Publishing Board. The course cards for classes in the B. T. U., Division came from the National B. T. U., Board. (By this time the Baptist Training Union had replaced the Baptist Young People's Union as the Sunday Evening program for the churches, and its work expanded to encompass all church members.) The question was raised as to the visibility of the Congress in a denominational program where the Congress as a denominational agency depended upon other agencies for its programs. Furthermore, the Congress was dealing with two separate Boards in accrediting its work.

Another problem arose in the administration of the leadership training curriculum since the courses offered in the B.T.U., Division, developed through the National B. T. U., Board, were not a part of the Standard Leadership Curriculum. Thus, persons who took "B. T. U., courses" were not given credits for these courses toward Certificates of Progress. There were extended discussions between the Congress and the two Boards. This resulted in the recognition of B. T. U., training credits as credits earned in "Denominational Courses" in the Standard Leadership Curriculum. It also resulted in a wording on the credit cards and Certificates issued in the Congress which stated that credits were given by the Congress in cooperation with the two Boards and the International Council of Religious Education. Thus, there was visibility for the Congress, recognition for its peculiar role in the denomination Christian education program, and integration of all study work into one denomination system.

2. Certificates of Progress.

In 1939 the Congress had developed its first "Graduating Class." But the people did not stop attending the Congress because they received diplomas. In the same way, persons who received the first, second and third Certificates of Progress did not stop attending the Congress upon receipt of their Certificates. So, the Congress developed a special Advanced Certificate, and a Certificate of Achievement, given by the Congress to persons who had gone beyond the requirements for Certificates of Progress in the Standard Leadership curriculum administered denominationally through the Sunday School Publishing Board.

3. **The increasing exposure and visibility of Christian education led States and Districts, as well as local churches, to step up their efforts at leadership training.**

What once were State and District Sunday School Conventions, and B. T. U., Conventions, now became Sunday School and B. T. U., Congresses, patterned after the National Congress. These Congresses were certified through the Sunday School Publishing Board. In response to the Board's efforts to expand its programs, institutes were conducted in selected areas, using staff persons from the Sunday School Publishing Board and the National Baptist Training Union Board. As part of this program the Sunday School Publishing Board offered subsidy to State Conventions which would appoint full-time Directors of Christian Education. The Board also appointed a Director of Field Work to coordinate the program. The Board produced manuals for the guidance of states in setting up their Christian education programs, as well as manuals and denominational supplements which outlined the Standard Leadership Curriculum.

4. **The Sunday School Publishing Board added to its professional staff in Christian education.**

By 1950 there were seven professional staff persons in the Department of Christian education, in addition to professionals retained as writers of literature and other curriculum resources. The National B. T. U., Board also expanded its professional staff, whose time was shared between producing literature, materials and manuals, and in conducting training courses in the field.

5. **Themes developed in the Congress for the Four-Year programs were being used throughout the denomination in states, districts and local churches.**

The Sunday School Publishing Board and the National B. T. U., Board were represented on the Four-Year Program Commissions of the Congress, which developed these themes. In the Commission meetings attention was not only given to ideas represented in the themes, but also to the solution of problems as the Congress and the Boards responded to the opportunities open to their respective areas of activity to improve Christian education in the denomination.

The result of this activity was that Christian education in the Congress and in the Convention was based on substantive approaches on the part of all of the agencies which were working together as a team. Although the independence of the respective units was established in the constitution of the Congress, as a practical matter it was essential to cooperate for the good of the educational programs in the churches.

It was "profits" in the Sunday School Publishing Board which made this expansion possible. It was the balancing of the Congress budget which made possible its services. But basic to both was the support of a grassroots constituency who saw to it that staff people from the Boards and officials in the Congress were invited to meetings, to speak, to counsel, and to lift the level of Christian education in the Convention and its churches.

But in 1949 the National Baptist Convention directed that profits from the Sunday School Publishing Board be used toward remodeling and operating the National Baptist Bath House and Hotel in Hot Springs, Arkansas, in addition to maintaining the Convention's commitments for the American Baptist Theological Seminary, the National Baptist Missionary Training School, and providing services to the Convention through printing of the National Baptist Voice, minutes, and other services. The result was a cutback in the Christian education programs through the Board, and a retreat to the Leadership Education program as the primary educational activity of the Board.

But, during the period 1943-50 some developments of importance took place. The role of the Sunday School Publishing Board and the National B. T. U., Board as "service units" to the Congress was established. Staff persons from the Sunday School Publishing Board and the B. T. U., Board were made available to serve the Congress. The primary example of this was the appointment of Miss Mildred L. McTyre as Director of Children's work for the Board. Miss McTyre was assigned to assist the Children's Division of the Congress in whatever ways were needed, as a part of her responsibility and employment with the Board. In this position Miss McTyre laid the plans and organized the first Laboratory School for Children's Workers, held in Louisville, Kentucky, in 1950. As professional staff grew in the Boards, these persons were made available to serve the needs of the Congress, in addition to carrying their responsibilities for Christian education activity through the Boards.

Another important development was the assistance given by the Congress and the Boards in promoting each other's activities. Announcements concerning Congress meetings, programs and activities were carried in the literature of the Boards. These announcements were also included in information sent to all of the Sunday Schools and Baptist Training Unions on the mailing lists of the Boards. In turn, the Congress offered in plenary session an opportunity for representatives of the Boards to make progress reports, and to encourage the use of the programs and materials being developed through the boards. The Congress agreed to restrict access to its list of textbooks and other resources used in its programs; the

Boards in turn agreed to furnish a supply of textbooks adequate to the needs of the Congress, but with due regard for the ability of the Boards to sell these materials and recover their investments.

There were evidences of growth in these years. Increasing numbers of States and Districts followed the basic curriculum of the Sunday School Publishing Board, and the program themes of the Congress. Congress and Board leaders gained exposure to the constituency in ways which complemented the efforts of each other. Congress leaders were involved in the work of the International Council of Religious Education, working alongside representatives of the Boards in the work of the Council. The President of the Congress was active in the work of other agencies, enhancing the visibility of the Congress both inside and outside the denomination.

These developments would not have been possible without the support of Dr. Jernagin, Dr. Townsend and Dr. Isaac. Credit must also be given to Dr. W. R. Murray and Dr. J. W. Gayden, Chairman of the Sunday School Publishing Board and National B. T. U., Board, respectively. In 1943 one would have thought that the independence of the Congress and the Boards would signal a long period of controversy and strife. Instead, there developed a model for cooperation between agencies acting independently of each other, yet in cooperation with each other, for serving the needs of a common constituency.

From 1950 to 1960

With the Four-Year Program, 1950-53, which began in Louisville, Kentucky, the Congress began the Laboratory School for Children's Workers. The plan at the time was to add a major new activity to the Congress curriculum as a feature of each new Four-Year Program. The planning was to be done cooperatively by the Congress and the Boards, with leadership either provided by or supported by persons in a professional position in a denominational agency. Miss McTyre, who was Director of Children's Work for the Sunday School Publishing Board, was thus assigned as Director of the Laboratory School. The effect of this arrangement would be to tie the developing Congress curriculum and services to the denominational effort in that area. Persons who used materials in the Churches would have an opportunity for exposure to the materials being produced by the Boards, and a vehicle to give their suggestions for improvements in the Board's program activities. This in turn would strengthen the Board's services to the churches. The Congress would provide this opportunity, and strengthen its own program.

However, the cut-back in the Christian education program in the Sunday School Publishing Board affected this plan. At the Sunday School Publishing Board Charles L. Dinkins resigned in order to accept the pastorate of a church. Then, Rev. Robert C. Wallace, who was Director of the Field Program for the Board, assumed the position of Secretary of the Christian Education Department of the Board. Miss McTyre soon resigned to take a position of faculty member at a College. Other members of the staff went to other positions, or assumed different responsibilities within the Board, mostly related to the production of literature for Missionary Societies, Vacation Church Schools, and Laymen's and Boys groups. These latter persons came under the supervision of Dr. George W. Harvey, Editor-in-Chief of the Board, but worked closely with the Christian Education Department, under Rev. Wallace.

This meant that the Congress was without the professional backing in the Sunday School Publishing Board and the National Baptist Training Union Board to make the plan for new projects work. For, in addition to setting up the respective projects, it was expected that the leadership in the Boards would keep the Congress faculty and workers informed on activities and developments in the field of Christian education and trends in the programs in the Boards, and to review lesson plans, text materials, and other resources to be used in the classes in the Congress. To meet this challenge several developments occurred in the Congress.

1. Beginning with the Four-Year Program of 1954 the Congress appointed Divisional Supervisors to do on a volunteer basis what was to have been done with professional leadership recruited from denominational agencies. Prior to 1954 each Congress Division was headed by a Leader, and sometimes an Assistant Leader, whose major activity was to coordinate records, reports, and other routines between the office of the Dean and the members of the Congress faculty. But these Leaders had no responsibility for the "content" of what went on in the classes. The Supervisors were appointed to do what was anticipated being done with denominational agency personnel. Coordinators and Assistant Coordinators became new titles for the Leaders and Assistant Leaders.

The Supervisors worked closely with the Dean, often at great personal sacrifice, since the Congress made no allocation for expenses of communication with the faculty members in the respective Divisions. The Supervisors also assumed responsibility for securing books and materials, attending meetings, and gaining exposure to trends in Christian education which they could pass on to their faculty, and enhance the quality of teaching in the Congress.

2. The Congress moved ahead in 1954 to add the Christian Education Administration Workshop to its program. This activity was selected

because, first, there were many Superintendents of Sunday Schools attending the Congress who had completed the requirements for the Certificates of Progress offered in the Congress; and, second, the Congress was making a major effort to give emphasis to the administration of Christian Education in the total church program, and not merely in administering Sunday Schools and Training Unions. The Congress called on Rev. Charles H. Fitzgerald, who was Professor of Christian Education at the American Baptist Theological Seminary, to direct this effort. An appeal was made to Seminary officials to "furnish" Rev. Fitzgerald to the Congress for this assignment. Thus the plan for leadership in a Congress activity to come from a person employed in a denominational agency was kept intact.

3. In 1958 the Congress added the Skill Shop to its curriculum. The basic design for the Skill Shop was developed in the Antioch District Congress in St. Louis, Missouri under Dr. Zaid D. Lenoir. Dr. Lenoir became the Director for this activity in the Congress. Prior to this appointment he was Supervisor of the Fine Arts Division of the Congress, which dealt primarily with courses in understanding pupils, teaching methods, and the application of music, art, drama, and the like, to teaching in Christian education programs in the church. This related the Skill Shop to the Fine Arts Division in the way that the Laboratory School was related to the Children's Division, and the Administration Workshop was related to the Administrative Division, of the Congress.

4. In 1955 the Congress observed its 50th Anniversary in a Golden Jubilee Session held in Atlantic City, N.J. For this session the Congress departed from its usual format for public programs, and presented three major speeches. Miss Lucie E. Campbell spoke on the Past of the Congress; Dr. A. M. Townsend spoke on the Congress in the Present; Rev. Charles L. Dinkins spoke on the Future of the Congress. One of the points made in the latter address was as to whether the Congress could continue to be effective as a "school in a suitcase," traveling from place to place without assembling in one place the resources necessary for an adequate leadership development program.

In the Sunday School Publishing Board by 1956 Dr. Harvey, Editor-in-Chief, had passed, and Rev. Robert C. Wallace, Secretary of Christian Education, had accepted a position as Executive Dean of Chicago Baptist Institute. In January, 1957, Charles L. Dinkins returned to the Sunday School Publishing Board as Director of Education and Assistant Secretary, carrying out responsibilities of Dr. Harvey and Rev. Wallace, but laying a foundation for a programmatic thrust which would coordinate Christian Education curriculum materials with Christian Education program designs for use in the local churches. The program was approved by the Board, but was never presented to the Convention.

In the First Quarter of 1958, the Sunday School Publishing Board produced an experimental series of quarterlies for children, based on the Uniform lessons. The series was tested in fifty Sunday Schools which were broadly representative of the churches served by the Board. The Series was presented at the Congress session of 1958 at Omaha, Nebraska, where sample copies were given to all persons enrolled in the Laboratory School and in the classes of the Children's Division, and criticisms were solicited.

Another important development took place. Since the Sunday School Publishing Board viewed its responsibility as serving the needs of the total church in organizing and carrying out its program of Christian education, the Board moved to establish a program and curriculum designed for this purpose. But, at the same time Southern Baptists and American (formerly Northern) Baptists continued to support missionaries, field workers and others who instructed people in National Baptist churches. These instructors presented the programs and curriculum materials of their sponsors. This problem was presented to leaders in the respective denominations, and discussions held. In June, 1959, at the Congress session held in Memphis, Tennessee, representatives of the American and Southern Baptist mission agencies met with representatives of the Sunday School Publishing Board and the National B. T. U., Board to develop a policy that permitted National Baptist materials to be promoted alongside materials from the other Baptist groups in their missionary and educational programs serving churches affiliated with the National Baptist Convention.

In 1959 Dr. A. M. Townsend, Secretary of the Sunday School Publishing Board passed, and at the next session of the National Baptist Convention, in San Francisco, California, Dr. D. C. Washington was elected Executive Director of the Sunday School Publishing Board. Charles L. Dinkins resigned from the Sunday School Publishing Board to accept a position as President of Owen College, Memphis, Tennessee. Then, Dr. Jesse Jai McNeil returned to the Sunday School Publishing Board as Director of Publications.

In the National Baptist Training Union Board, Dr. E. W. D. Isaac was succeeded by Dr. Roland Smith, then by Rev. C. R. Williams. This Board continued its traditional programs, but Rev. Williams offered to and received from the Congress valuable suggestions which were mutually helpful.

In the Congress, the death of Dr. Jernagin in 1958, meant a vacancy in the Presidency of the Congress. Dr. O. Clay Maxwell was elected President, and Dr. Martin Luther King, Jr., was elected Vice-President. In

1960, Dr. A. Franklin Fisher, Dean of the Congress, passed. He was succeeded by Dr. Horatio S. Hill, Assistant Dean, and Director of the Baptist Educational Center of New York City. Charles L. Dinkins became an Assistant Dean, serving along with Dr. A. McEwen Williams.

Thus the Congress entered the Sixties with the new set of personalities to influence it. Dr. J. H. Jackson was President of the National Baptist Convention, U.S.A., Inc. Dr. O. Clay Maxwell was President, and Dr. Martin Luther King, Jr., Vice-President of the Congress. Dr. Horatio S. Hill was Dean of the Congress, with Revs. A. McEwen Williams and Charles L. Dinkins as Assistant Deans. Dr. D. C. Washington was Executive Director of the Sunday School Publishing Board, with Dr. Jesse Jai McNeil as Director of Publications. Dr. C. R. Williams was Executive Secretary of the National Baptist Training Union Board.

From 1960 to 1970

The decades of the Sixties saw changes taking place inside and outside of Congress which were to affect its development and programs.

1. It was the era of civil rights advancements and improvements in the technology which served the needs of people. It was an era where the Congress had benefited from mass movements by trains, which meant that the movement of delegations was regulated, the trend now was toward travel by using buses, private cars, and planes. As accommodations opened in hotels, there was a lessening of dependence upon private housing for Congress delegates. The opening of hotels also meant access to meeting rooms, a fact which was especially important in cities where access to public schools or college facilities was not possible for use as Congress classes. As the economic status of many messengers improved, they came to the Congress, although not "sent" by the local churches, using vacation leaves and their private resources for the purpose. This meant that many persons in the Congress felt less of an obligation to attend all of the classes and public meetings.

2. It was an era which continued the urbanization of the Black people. More resources were made available to the people to insure their participation in the life of their respective communities. Voting rights, public accommodations, and other advances expanded the horizons open to people, and generated leadership in local communities and affected the leadership patterns in local churches. Many churches bought or built new facilities which contained space for expanded Christian education programs and activities.

3. It was an era which saw the strengthening of the influence of the National Baptist Convention in the Congress. There was no attempt to

control the program or appointments of persons to serve in the Congress, but there was a greater emphasis on Convention approval of Congress officers, and on reporting of Congress activity to the Convention Board of Directors and President.

4. There were changes in the mainstream of Christian education activity. In the early 1960s fourteen denominations that were members of the Division of Christian Education of the National Council of Churches authorized the Cooperative Curriculum Project, which resulted in the publication of "The Church's Educational Ministry: A Curriculum Plan", with the following as the statement of the objective of Christian Education:

> The objective for Christian education is that all persons be aware of God through his self-disclosure, especially his redeeming love as revealed in Jesus Christ, and that they respond in faith and love—to the end that they may know who they are and what their human situation means, grow as sons of God rooted in the Christian community, live in the Spirit of God in every relationship, fulfill their common discipleship in the world, and abide in the Christian hope.

These denominations, which had cooperated in the production of Uniform and Graded lessons for use in churches, began to examine their own curriculum designs and the supportive leadership materials and programs. They also began to look at the distinctives in their denominational histories, doctrines and programs. The result was a new pattern of curriculum design, and leadership development programs and activities to support them. There was a decline in emphasis on the Standard Leadership Curriculum for training of church workers in favor of the use of leadership materials which specifically coordinated with the new curriculum designs. Denominations which produced texts for the Standard Leadership Curriculum did not reprint these books when their supply became exhausted, resulting in a decline in the materials and resources available to service the Curriculum. Ultimately this led to the abandonment of the Standard Leadership Curriculum as an interdenominational leadership training system.

In the meantime, the Congress entered the 1960s with its basic plans in operation. In 1962 the Congress began the Jernagin Lecture Series. The plan was that this activity would accommodate those persons who had completed Certificates of Progress and who continued to come to the Congress, but were not interested in the Laboratory School, Administration Workshop or Skill Shop. The Jernagin Lecture Series would be "open-ended", in that there was to be no terminating point for completing this activity. The lectures would be based on contemporary topics and issues, and expose those attending to outstanding leaders in the field of Christian education. In 1962 the lecturer was from the Iliff School of Theology in Denver, where the Congress was being held. However, by 1964, Dr. Maxie S. Gordon and Dr. Maynard P. Turner, Jr., had become the lecturers, with their specific topics varying from year to year in line with contemporary issues and general congress themes.

In the 1950s the Congress changed its format from Sunday School courses in the mornings and B. T. U., courses in the afternoon. According to the format which resulted, classes in General, Administrative and Youth Divisions were held in the mornings, and classes in the Children's, Adult and Fine Arts Divisions were held in the afternoons. Special Projects, Ministers Seminars and Ministers' Wives groups met both morning and afternoon. This meant that a person attending the Congress could take two courses at a given session, and could conceivably secure a First Certificate of Progress in two years. The time could be cut if credits were earned in other Congresses or leadership training schools. Furthermore, the Third Certificate could be received in six years or less. Many persons were attending the Congress with Third Certificates already in hand.

It was a requirement of the Standard Leadership Curriculum that a person spend as much time on outside study relating to a class as that person spent in the class. It was not possible to meet this standard in the Congress format.

In 1966 the Congress changed its format to conduct all class work in the standard courses in the morning study period, and to use afternoons for Discussion Groups developed in the six Divisions of the Congress. Thus, a person taking a morning course was required to attend an afternoon discussion group in the same Division. The discussion groups were based on presentations made in the morning general assemblies. A Divisional lecturer would capsule the emphases in the morning general assembly and relate them to the interest of persons in the respective Divisions; then Discussion Leaders would carry on the discussions in small groups. Recognition of participation was by a sticker attached to the credit card, thus validating it.

To accommodate this arrangement the morning sessions presented major addresses according to the following plan: Tuesday, Dean's Keynote address; Wednesday, major presentation by guest speaker; Thursday, President's annual address; Friday, major presentation by guest speaker. Evening sessions were based on the following plan: Monday, Pre-Congress Musical; Tuesday, Welcome Program, Sermon; Wednesday, Missionary or Educational Sermon; Thursday, Youth Rally; Friday, Booker T. Washington Night. Saturday morning was Commencement, followed by the meeting of the Congress Board.

In addition, the Sunday School Publishing Board produced for the Congress a study guide book for each annual session, covering the congress theme for that year. The writers were selected and paid by the Congress. In early years the Congress purchased these guides for inclusion in delegates' kits; later, the Board produced the guides on behalf of the Congress and recovered its costs from sales. (The Board thus could also service the needs of State, District Congress and churches throughout the year, since the Congress had no means of handling sales of the publication.)

While these changes were taking place in the Congress, changes were also taking place in the Sunday School Publishing Board. Dr. Jesse Jai McNeil introduced a Graded Lesson Series for Sunday schools, but the costs were not recovered in corresponding sales, and the series was discontinued. However, it did introduce the idea of graded lessons for Black Baptist churches. Dr. Maynard P. Turner, Jr., succeeded Dr. McNeil as Director of Publications. Although the Christian Education Department of the Board was under professional leadership for a short period, the Board continued to provide services to the Congress through Dr. D. C. Washington, Executive Director, who assigned staff persons to respond to requests from the Congress. Dr. C. R. Williams, Executive Secretary of the National B. T. U., Board, also responded in this manner. Both the Sunday School Publishing Board and the National B. T. U., Board were represented on the Four-Year Program Commission of the Congress, and participated in all of the developments in the Congress. The Sunday School Publishing Board and B. T. U., Board provided the textbooks for the Congress sessions. The Congress tried to protect the Boards to guarantee that they recovered costs for these books, but published lists of textbooks made it possible for other vendors to compete with the Boards for sales.

In the meantime the Congress was feeling the effects of the shortage of textbook materials. A suggestion came from the National Baptist Convention that the Congress should meet this problem by securing its own writers. But, the absence of text material meant that many instructors produced their own lectures and outlines and sold them in their classes. This material was for the most part unrelated to any program promoted through the denomination.

This raised the question of the integration of Congress materials into the total denominational effort in Christian education, and the role of the Congress in "policing" and "protecting" denominational programs.

The decline in the Standard Leadership Curriculum, however, had little effect on the Congress or the leadership education program of the Sunday School Publishing Board. Courses continued as usual, in spite of the lack of textbooks and the absence of the interdenominational program.

Administration continued as before. Only the National Baptist Convention and the Progressive National Baptist Convention were now using the basic Standard Leadership Curriculum program. The separation of the Conventions, however, did not present a problem, since there apparently developed no issues involving the interchange of credits between the two groups.

In the Congress, other changes were taking place in its personnel. Prior to the 1965 session of the Congress Dr. E. C. Estell passed, and Dr. E. A. Freeman was elected Vice-President. In 1968, in Chattanooga, Tennessee, Dr. Maxwell resigned as President because of his health. In that session Dr. Freeman was elected President; Dr. James B. Cayce, Vice President; Dr. T. Oscar Chapelle, Director General; and Dr. I. H. Henderson, Jr., Associate Director General.

In his first annual message to the Congress in 1969 in Miami, Florida, Dr. Freeman recommended that the President's Annual Message be delivered on Thursday night, giving an opportunity for people in the host city to hear the message, which "will deal with the heart, scope and general purpose of the Congress' work". With Youth Night established as Friday Night, Dr. Freeman stated that "our morning plenary sessions can then deal more with the academic and technical aspects of our work". He also pledged "that the Congress shall remain an auxiliary to the parent body and serve only as its arm in Christian education, according to the constitution of both bodies."

In 1962, Charles L. Dinkins was named Associate Dean of the Congress, and Dr. Horace N. Mays, of California, was named Assistant Dean. One of Dr. Mays' major contributions was the development of the plan for Discussion Groups begun in 1966, and the training of the persons to be used in this phase of Congress activity. In 1969 Dean Horatio S. Hill resigned, and Charles L. Dinkins served as Dean for one year. During this year there were discussions on the future of the Congress and its relationships with the Sunday School Publishing Board and the National B. T. U., Board. Dr. Freeman and Dr. Washington led in these discussions, which were as important to the future of the Congress as any discussions at any other period in the history of the Congress. The result was that in 1970 Dr. Maynard P. Turner, Jr., who was in the Sunday School Publishing Board as Director of Publications, became Dean of the Congress. Also, a room at the Sunday School Publishing Board was set apart to store and maintain Congress records.

Thus the Congress entered the seventies with a new set of personalities to influence it. Dr. J. H. Jackson was President of the National Baptist Convention, U.S.A., Inc. Dr. E. A. Freeman was President of the Congress, with Dr. James B. Cayce as Vice President, Dr. T. Oscar Chappelle, Sr. as Director General, and Dr. I. H. Henderson, Jr., as Associate Director General. Dr. Maynard P. Turner, Jr., was serving as Dean, with Dr. Robert E. Penn, Associate Dean, and Dr. A. McEwen Williams and Dr. Horace N. Mays as Assistant Deans, Charles L. Dinkins continued as Secretary of the Congress Program Commission. Dr. D. C. Washington was Executive Director of the Sunday School Publishing Board, and Dr. C. R. Williams, was Executive Secretary of the National B. T. U., Board.

From 1970 to 1980

The coming of Dr. Turner as Dean brought significant additions to the program of the Congress. As has been noted, beginning in 1950, a special project activity was added to the Congress in each new Four-Year Program. These included the Laboratory School for Children's Workers (1950), the Christian Education Administration Workshop (1954), the Skill Shop (1958), the Jernagin Lecture Series (1962), and the change in format to Discussion Groups in the afternoons following Congress Lectures in morning plenary sessions (1966). However, for the 1970-73 Four-Year Program no new projects had been developed, or were scheduled for development. Dr. Turner moved to accommodate the increasing interest of the people in special fields of endeavor, and in 1971 introduced several new Projects. These were the Lucie E. Campbell Church Music Workshop, the Church Secretaries Workshop, the Contemporary Ministries Workshop, and the Christian Youth on the College Campus Workshop. Later, Workshops were added in Foreign Missions, The Church Library, and in Aging Successfully. These Projects, with the addition of Youth Rally and the Jernagin Lecture Series, were organized into a Special Projects Division in the Congress. The other Special Projects were related to one of the other Divisions of the Congress, such as the Laboratory School, Children's Division, Administration Workshop, Administrative Division, Skill Shop, and Fine Arts Division. Each of these Special Projects met mornings and afternoons, except Youth Rally, which permitted persons to enroll in morning classes and attend Youth Rally in the afternoons instead of Discussion Groups.

The entrance requirements for participation in the Special Projects were defined. It was also required that persons attend four years in order to receive a special certificate for completion of the Special Project. In the case of the Jernagin Lecture Series, which was not a project with a termination point, a plan was developed to recognize at intervals participation over a number of years.

In the meantime the Congress was beginning to feel strongly the effects of the discontinuance of the Standard Leadership Curriculum as an interdenominational training program. In 1973, in Dallas, Texas, President Freeman in his address pointed out the problems before the Congress. He noted that the Congress provided opportunity for leadership training, for inspiration of church workers and for bi-lateral communications between the denominational Christian educational program and the constituency of the Congress. He pointed to problems the Congress was facing in the proliferation of course offerings, in the lack of adequate textbooks and resource materials, and the need for maximizing the number of people served by the Congress. He noted that there were resources available to the Congress, including qualified and dedicated persons who were associated with the Congress, but that there were problems with some resources, including the adequacy of physical facilities offered by different cities which hosted the Congress, and the financial resources available to the Congress to enable it to carry out its functions.

In his message Dr. Freeman proposed a change in format which would allow the Congress to close on Friday Night. He also proposed that the Dean, in cooperation with the Sunday School Publishing Board, recommend textbook materials for courses for which there were no textbooks. He called for evaluation of the Special Projects, and the development of Mini-Congresses, sponsored by the Congress in areas where the full Congress is not likely to meet, helping to "develop Christian education work in these areas which are now under-developed either for the Congress, or for the Sunday School and Baptist Training Union Boards, or for their own programs." Finally, he called for an in-depth evaluation of the Congress effort "in order to determine whether the Congress is effectively serving and keeping pace with the mainstream of Christian Education, and as to whether the constituency is ready for some needed changes." He suggested that the Congress should work simultaneously on two tracks: first, to retain the present system of courses and textbooks; second, to develop more sophisticated types of training.

In 1974, in Detroit, Michigan, Dr. Freeman expanded on the Mini-Congress concept, and reported on the Mini-Congress conducted in Charlotte, N.C. in March, 1974.

Dean Penn was given the responsibility of coordinating the evaluation of the Congress program, and developing solutions. In 1974 Dr. Penn proposed that a special Curriculum Study Consultation be developed to carry out the assignment. In February, 1975, the Congress Executive Committee approved the plan, and allocated funds to underwrite the effort. The Steering Committee was composed of Dean Penn, Associate Dean Turner, Dr. Charles L. Dinkins, Secretary of the Program Commission, Dr. Odell McGlothian, Sr., Director of Publications, representing the Sunday School Publishing Board, and Dr. T. H. Rankin, Sr., representing the National B. T. U., Board. Others in the Consultation included representatives of the Congress Executive Committee, the Dean's Official Staff, the Sunday School Publishing Board, the National B. T. U., Board, and additional persons who were asked to serve because of their special interests and talents in relation to the objectives of the Consultation. The first meeting of this Consultation was held in Nashville, Tennessee, in March, 1976.

In the meantime there were changes that were taking place in the Convention which affected the Congress. In its session in St. Louis, Missouri, in September, 1975, the Convention voted to change the name of the Congress from the National Sunday School and B.T.U. Congress, to the National Baptist Congress of Christian Education. The Convention further voted a change in the titles of the President and Vice-President of the Congress to Superintendent and Assistant Superintendent, respectively. An additional change placed responsibility for arrangements for the annual sessions of the Congress in the hands of a committee appointed by and responsible to the Convention, with the Convention signing necessary contracts with local Convention Bureaus and agencies for space, housing, and other accommodations for the Congress. The Convention would also arrange for the Pre-Convention Musical Program, the Souvenir Program Book, the Exhibit Area, relieving local entertainment committees of these responsibilities.

The 1976 Curriculum Study Consultation reviewed the Congress format, the Congress curriculum, and the theological and educational undergirding for Christian education. Also there was a review of some of the forms in which Christian education took place and special programs that were conducted in representative National Baptist churches. Special attention was given to a presentation of the denominational Christian education design, by representatives of the Sunday School Publishing Board and the National Baptist Training Union Board. At the conclusion of the Consultation resolutions were adopted to be presented to the Executive Board of the Congress, as follows:

1. That the Congress study its curriculum as it relates to the patterns and structures of educational programs now being conducted in the National Baptist Convention and recommended for use in its member churches.
2. That the Congress seek to initiate a program to study and redefine Christian education as it related to the programs and causes of the National Baptist Convention.
3. That the Congress arrange a special procedure for orientation of prospective faculty members and substitute teachers, beginning in 1977, and that participation be mandatory for prospective faculty.

4. That the Curriculum Study be continued as an on-going activity until the task which has been assigned to it has been completed.
5. That in the light of the former Standard Leadership Curriculum, we study the accreditation process of credits earned in the present Leadership Education curriculum as it relates to the Congress.

These findings were adopted by the Congress Board in June, 1976 in San Francisco, California. At this session Dean Penn resigned his position in the Congress because of his health. Dr. Maynard P. Turner, Jr., living in Nassau, Bahamas since 1974, was named Dean of the Congress. Dr. A. McEwen Williams was named Associate Dean; Dr. Horace N. Mays and Dr. Joseph H. Williams were named Assistant Deans. Dr. Penn passed in 1976, and Dr. Mays passed in 1977. Dr. S. J. Royal was then appointed Assistant Dean.

In the meantime, Dr. D. C. Washington, Executive Director of the Sunday School Publishing Board, passed in October, 1974, and was succeeded by Mrs. Cecelia Nabrit Adkins, daughter of the late Dr. J. M. Nabrit, former Secretary of the National Baptist Convention, U.S.A., Inc., and President of the American Baptist Theological Seminary. Dr. C. R. Williams resigned as Executive Secretary of the National B. T. U. Board and his responsibilities were assumed by Dr. T. H. Rankin, Sr., Board Chairman, and the office staff. Mrs. Vada P. Felder continued as Director of Publications.

The findings of the 1976 Consultation were presented to Dr. J. H. Jackson, President of the National Baptist Convention, U.S.A., Inc. At a meeting with Dr. Jackson in Dallas, Texas, in September, 1976, the question was raised as to what the Convention expects of the Congress in terms of its role in the Convention and the scope of Congress activity. In a subsequent meeting with President Jackson in Hot Springs, Arkansas, in January, 1977, he responded as follows:

"We have entrusted the work and leadership in the educational phase of our denomination to our Congress of Christian Education. We have also given to them the freedom and latitude to choose the materials and to organize their resources to the best of their ability. Our request to them is as follows:

1. That as nearly as possible, in preparing their materials, they will speak to the needs of the denomination.
2. They will as much as possible, encourage our writers not only to produce study materials, but to produce service manuals and books that will interpret religion in the light of the thought patterns of the present day.
3. We also desire some resources or courses to create a pool of

leaders from which the Church may draw future deacons, choir directors, and other essential persons for the service and progress of the church."

With this background statement from the Convention, the March, 1977 Curriculum Study Consultation considered the Mission, Goals, and Objectives of the Congress, and began discussion on ways to implement these. The summary of Mission, Goals and Objectives is as follows:

THE CONGRESS MISSION: To develop standards and criteria for Christian Education in the National Baptist Convention, U.S.A., Inc., and to give visibility to these standards.

GOAL—1. To increase opportunities for exposure of the Standards for Christian Education for the constituency of the Convention.

Objective—1. To increase attendance at the Annual Sessions of the Congress to 13,000 messengers by 1980.

Objective—2. To support the efforts of State and District Congresses to increase opportunities for reaching people with exposure to the Christian Education standards.

Objective—3. To sponsor efforts to initiate and extend opportunities for exposure to the Congress in areas of the constituency where exposure is now limited.

Objective—4. To stimulate the production and use of materials and methods to embody standards of Christian education for local churches, associations, and states.

GOAL—2. To increase the efficiency and effectiveness of persons in the use of Standards for Christian Education in the National Baptist Convention.

Objective—1. To develop a basic systematic program of study for persons who serve in positions of leadership in churches.

Objective—2. To develop supportive resources, including textbooks, for study and guidance of persons essential to the service and progress of the church.

Objective—3. To cooperate with agencies and Boards in the production of service manuals for the guidance of people who lead in the work of the church and its structured organizations.

GOAL—3. To increase the number and availability of persons appropriately qualified and equipped from which the local church can draw for the service and progress of the church.

Objective—1. To develop a basic program for enhancing the understanding and appreciation of members for the meaning of Church membership, and for their orientation in the history, doctrines and mission of the church.

Objective—2. To cooperate in the production of materials to support this program.

GOAL—4. To increase the number of people who can be available to the Congress and serve as "enablers" and "facilitators" in the accomplishment of its mission.

Objective—1. To develop in-service training programs for faculty persons to increase their efficiency in contributing to the programs of the Congress.

Objective—2. To identify, recruit and provide orientation for new faculty.

GOAL—5. To develop resources necessary to carry out the mission of the Congress.

Objective—1. To provide a resource base which will support the budget necessary to carry out the mission of the Congress.

Objective—2. To provide the personnel which will provide support services necessary to carry out the mission of the Congress.

Objective—3. To provide the facilities and equipment which will provide support to carry out the mission of the Congress.

Objective—4. To provide the management of resources available to carry out the mission of the Congress.

It was pointed out that further delineation of these goals and objectives are necessary for the development of specific goals for administration, program, curriculum and finance. Steps were taken in this direction, but because of budget limitations the third meeting of the Consultation has not yet been held. Interim activity is being coordinated by Dean Turner and Dr. Dinkins.

In the effort to extend the Congress' range of service and improve its fiscal position, special effort has been made to promote increased attendance at Congress sessions. Finances for the Congress are tied to "representations" by Sunday Schools, Training Unions and other groups. Congress officers have appeared in various sections of the country, and communications have been sent to churches and church workers. The constituency is encouraged to invite Congress leaders as guests, and thus enhance the visibility of the Congress, and promote attendance.

In the Sunday School Publishing Board the appointment of Dr. Amos Jones, Jr., to the position of Secretary of the Christian Education Department, has brought professional leadership to the Board to develop and coordinate the Board's program activities. In December, 1979, a conference of State Directors of Christian Education was held. At this meeting these persons were exposed to some of the trends in Christian Education, and to the program which will be promoted through the Board.

Dean Turner has returned to Nashville, Tennessee, where he serves as Executive Secretary of the Tennessee Baptist Missionary and Educational Convention. There is advantage in the Dean of the Congress being in the same city with the Sunday School Publishing Board and the National B. T. U., Board, in that it affords a better opportunity for cooperation and coordination in the development of the denominational effort in Christian education as it serves the needs of the Churches.

And so, as the Congress completes seventy-five years of service, and looks forward to the eighties, persons are in place to influence its development. Dr. J. H. Jackson is President of the National Baptist Convention, U. S. A., Inc. Dr. E. A. Freeman is Superintendent of the Congress, with Dr. T. O. Chappelle as Assistant Superintendent. Dr. I. H. Henderson, Jr., as Director General, and Dr. Avery Aldridge, as Associate Director General. Mrs. Bessie S. Estell is Secretary and Dr. J. C. Oliver is Treasurer. Dr. Maynard P. Turner, Jr., serves as Dean, with Dr. A. McEwen Williams as Associate Dean, Dr. Joseph Williams and Dr. S. J. Royal as Assistant Deans. Dr. Charles L. Dinkins serves as Secretary of the Congress Program Commission. Mrs. Cecelia N. Adkins serves as Executive Director of the Sunday School Publishing Board, with Dr. Amos Jones as Director of the Christian Education Department, and Dr. Odell McGlothian as Director of Publications. Dr. T. H. Rankin, Sr., serves as Chairman of the National B. T. U., Board.

What Of The Future?

The seventy-five year history of the Congress shows how this organization has responded to the needs of its constituency, and to the forces inside and outside the organization that have affected it. The Congress has become an "institution". Institutions outlive their founders, and those who serve at any given time develop the policies and programs to guarantee their relevance for the present and succeeding generations. Institutions are made stronger as they attract resources to help fulfill their mission. Institutions are validated by the people they serve.

Any attempt to forecast the future would be pure speculation. However, there are some issues that the Congress must address as it faces the future. These have been anticipated in the work of the Curriculum Study Consultation, and are repeated here for emphasis only:

1. The Congress is a one-week Leadership Training School. The total denominational effort in Christian education is a year-round activity, and must be anchored in the Sunday School Publishing Board and the National B. T. U. Board. Checks and balances, and the use of the resources of each agency to enhance the work and activity of the others can only

build added strength into the total denominational program as it serves churches and their needs.

2. The program of the Congress is growing, and its execution requires concern for accommodations for classrooms, logistics, schedules, transportation, and other concerns which affect the ability of the Congress to function. This means adopting program designs well in advance of future sessions, in order that accommodations can be adequate.

3. The Congress is being attended more and more by people who are not the traditional "messengers", but who are on vacation, in families that travel together, and who "drop in" on Congress activities that interest them. This may suggest informal activities, exhibits, and single-session-type programs which people related to Christian education can attend as an alternative to formal class study and progress through a structured curriculum.

4. The Congress is a "hand operation", and is affected by long lines at registration and other problems which develop while serving large numbers of people in a short period of time. This suggests that the Congress find ways, in cooperation with the Boards, to use modern technology, including computer science, to apply to such Congress activities as communications, registrations, and the like, based on standardization of Congress procedures.

5. The Congress depends for its finances on "representations" by Sunday Schools, Training Unions, Churches, District and State Congresses, and other organizations. While increases in basic fees to these organizations may not be a problem, increasing costs of travel and maintenance for persons in attendance may in the future be a problem in the light of benefits received, requiring further adjustment in the Congress programs and schedules.

But perhaps speculation about the future can best be considered in how the Congress responds to changes that are taking place within the churches that are being served. The last twenty years have given a special kind of visibility to the Black church and its role in civil rights and social action. It may well be that the Black church will have to renew its emphasis on organization, administration, efficiency in carrying out its Mission, that gave us Schools, Colleges, and other institutions, and thus become a model for the Black community to strengthen itself through building and bringing strength to its institutions. Churches can be led to determine what to support through their own programs, what to support together through their collective efforts with other churches, and what to support through subsidy and contributions to other agencies. People who have been "inspired" through the rhetoric developed in the churches, now must be led to appreciate the application of sound principles of planning, management and evaluation to the work carried on in the churches.

The Congress has demonstrated that it has the capacity to respond to changing needs and changing opportunity. The Convention has demonstrated its capacity to mold and maintain people into a strong organizational unit. In seventy-five years the Congress has come a long way. It has not "arrived," nor will it ever "arrive." The strength of its future is in its capacity to respond to its opportunity in the light of its mission, and serve the needs of its constituency.

NOTES

NOTES

NOTES

NOTES

NOTES

NOTES